SUPERB MAINE SOUPS

Innovative Recipes from Simple to Sumptuous

Cynthia Finnemore Simonds

Photographs by Randall Smith

Drawings by the Author

Down East Books

ISBN: 0-89272-738-1   (13-digit) 978-089272-738-4

Design concept by Chilton Creative
Printed in China   (RPS)

2   4   5   3

Library of Congress Cataloging-in-Publication Data

Simonds, Cynthia Finnemore, 1966–
Superb maine soups : innovative recipes from simple to sumptuous / Cynthia
Finnemore Simonds ; photographs by Randall Smith ; drawings by the author.
       p.   cm.
Includes index.
ISBN-13: 978-0-89272-738-4 (trade pbk. : alk. paper)
1. Soups.   2. Cookery–Maine.   I. Title.
TX757.S543 2007
641.8'13–dc22
2007011658

BOOKS·MAGAZINE·ONLINE
w w w . d o w n e a s t . c o m

Distributed to the trade by National Book Network

This book is dedicated to the special men in my life who know how to lead. To my father, Fred Finnemore, who taught me to love jazz and showed me how to fox-trot as a little girl by standing on the tops of his feet. To my husband, Sherwood, who dances me into happiness every day. To our son, Travis Simonds, who is growing into a fine gentleman who can glide me across a dance floor. To Campbell Searle, a dance partner extraordinaire, to whom I will always respond "Yes!" when he asks me to dance. And to Todd Finnemore, the best brother in the world, who is just beginning his dance. Lead on!

Dreams defined are possible
In a life lived deliberately
—CFS

CONTENTS

Introduction
8

Soup Beginnings
12

Clear Soups
21

Creamy Soups
31

Stews
47

Chowders and Other Thick Soups
59

Chilled Soups
77

Dessert Soups
85

Over the Top and On the Side
93

Appendix: Specialty Products from Maine Producers
102

Index
104

INTRODUCTION

The fragrance of bubbling, warm soup can hypnotize the strongest among us to extend a bowl and pull up a chair to the table. These days of hurried meals and convenience foods have caught up to us. It's time to slow down, to appreciate once again the flavors that can come from our own kitchen in surprisingly little time.

You'll find ideas and recipes here that allow you to make a quick batch of hearty soup—or prepare a few ingredients in the morning before work, plug in your slow cooker, and come home to a delicious, healthful meal. With very little planning, you can enjoy additive- and preservative-free meals that are full of flavor and tempt even the tiniest tummies.

Find time. Sit back. Savor your food. Linger with your family, and enjoy what you have before you. It's time for a bowl of your favorite soup.

Thrifty, Frugal, Yankee

I grew up in a home where my mom always baked bread, roasted chickens, and made her own stock. Those were the times when it was expected that meals would be homemade. I can remember begging her at the grocery store to buy TV dinners. They were a novelty. How cool it seemed then to have all your food in one handy tray! These days the norm for most families is to purchase convenience foods. They pick up prepackaged potatoes, refrigerator biscuits, and frozen entrées. Why not take a moment to break this cycle?

I've learned through my frugal Yankee roots to freeze any leftover goodies that I can use to flavor my soups. My friend Robin is the best I know at organizing her leftovers. By labeling gallon-size ziplock plastic freezer bags, she keeps her onion ends, extra green beans, turkey bones, and squash peelings in the freezer, ready to use. Every day she casually tosses extra bits and pieces into the appropriate bag. When the veggie-peel bag gets full, it's time to make soup. If she needs to make stock, she simply takes out whichever bags she wants to use. The leftovers go into a pot of water, and her soup is started before she even has to go to her pantry. This is a great way to economize when making soups, because freezing leftovers lets us use up the extra bits that would otherwise get thrown away or composted. Adding mashed potato or winter squash, for example, will thicken the broth and enhance its flavor.

One of my favorite ways to start a soup is by using leftover chicken bones. Whenever we finish a roast chicken or turkey—whether it came from the market's rotisserie or was roasted in our oven—we freeze the bones with any meat still left on them. At soup making time, I just place them in a pot, cover them with water, and simmer for a couple of hours to extract all the flavorful goodness. I throw in herb stems that I've saved, vegetable peelings from the freezer, whole cloves of garlic, and voilà! My soup is well on its way to being full of flavor.

The best soups incorporate layers of flavor. It's important to have a balance of ingredients so one doesn't dominate your dish. You want to taste the delicate herbs alongside the hearty meat or creamy cheeses. Sample as you go. It is the best way to keep the flavors balanced.

Soups are often meat based, but vegetables are a wonderful alternative. We have several prepared commercial options to achieve the flavors of chicken, beef, seafood, or vegetables. Powdered bouillon comes in packets, in jars, and pressed into cubes. These are viable options for flavoring soups. Broth also comes in cans or coated paper containers. Bouillon pastes often come in jars, and most should be refrigerated.

Read the labels before you purchase bouillon or broth. Decide for yourself and your family what combination of ingredients will best suit you. Some brands are very high in sodium, although many offer low-salt and fat-free versions as well. Others contain MSG or starch. Whichever brand you choose, make sure to adjust your recipe to accommodate the amount of salt in the prepackaged bouillon or broth.

Starting from Scratch

Don't let it scare you: Starting from scratch is an easy way to create your own masterpieces in the kitchen. Soup is best when you bring together the flavors your family loves.

My favorite way to begin a soup is by making stock. Once it has simmered and settled, you're left with a delicious base from which to build the flavors of your soup.

Many people ask about the difference in flavor between fresh and frozen vegetables. Whenever you have the opportunity to purchase locally grown ingredients from a farmer's market or your corner market, take it! Fresh veggies are always the best, although frozen vegetables take a close second in flavor. Most often they are frozen at their peak of freshness, so they are ready to become a part of your soup as soon as they're out of the bag. Frozen vegetables can be added right into your bubbling pot just before you're ready to serve. They will cook in the last few minutes and be bright and colorful as you dish up your soup.

Herbs and spices are another story. When did you last purchase dried herbs? Do you remember when you bought that can of ground black pepper that is at the back of your spice shelf? If you aren't sure you bought those herbs and spices within the last six months, out they go. Use fresh herbs whenever possible. Their flavor is brighter and more full-bodied. If you need to use dried herbs, purchase them in small quantities. Buying herbs and spices on the same day you pick up your vegetables will give your recipes an extra zing.

A wonderful thing about soups is that they can showcase the best local ingredients from one's home area. Here in Maine we have an active, enthusiastic farmer's market network (guides are available at the www.getrealgetmaine.com Web site). These open-air markets are the best places to find anything grown or produced locally, from fresh vegetables to wild mushrooms, specialty cheeses, condiments, and organic meats and eggs. The Maine Department of Agriculture, Food, and Rural Resources also publishes two helpful booklets: *Finding Maine Farmer's Markets: A Guide to Maine's Farmer's Markets* and *Finding Maine Foods and Farms: A Guide to Maine's Farms and Food Companies*.

Of course, Maine is famous for its lobster and other seafood. Aquaculture farms raise trout and salmon.

Local smokehouses produce golden smoked mussels, trout, cheeses, and other specialties. All of these are excellent additions to soups, and in the recipes that follow, I indulge in a little bit of local pride by specifying products from selected Maine producers. You can, of course, substitute equivalent ingredients, but I'd certainly encourage you to try the genuine Maine-made items first. On pages 102 and 103 you'll find information on how to order the specialty foods listed in my recipes.

Make These Recipes Your Own

One of my favorite things to do with cookbooks is to jot notes in them. When I make a recipe, I write in the date, whom I made it for or what occasion we celebrated, and what I did differently that time. I always smile as I turn the pages in my favorite cookbooks and am reminded of special times in years past.

I hope that you will use this book for yourself and for your family. Write in it. Make notes of what you like and how you changed things to fit your own taste. This is your book.

A Few Important Acknowledgments

I am so grateful to the people who have remained by my side through thick and thin. These are true friends, people who live on in my heart and my life.

Thanks go to my mother, Nancy Finnemore, for teaching me how to roast the bird and save the bones; to my friend Robin Schmidt for her wisdom, friendship and veggie-crunchy-ideals; to my friend Myrna Paye for her encouragement and generosity of spirit, and to Oprah for her excellence and inspiration—I'm on my way!

I thank Elizabeth and Travis for their constant cheers of "Go for it, Mom!" and my husband, Sherwood Olin, for his devotion to all things that make me happy.

Thanks also go to Cam Searle, who is always willing to go out and explore new restaurants or stay in and try new recipes, and to Donna Jean Kaiser, Susan Mayer, Michele Nardo, Kim McClain, Dianne Leavitt, Paula Schuster, Anne Marie Sacco, Paula Schuster, Carla Frisbee, Allison Linsley, Adele Gale, Gayle Yost, Molly Oliver, and Karyn Shippee—time is nonexistent and joy ever constant when I am with such good friends.

And a special thank-you goes to my editor, Karin Womer. I embrace your direction, appreciate your patience, and welcome your kindness.

—CFS

SOUP BEGINNINGS

When we pick the best local meats and produce, the freshest ingredients come together to become more than the sum of their parts. Begin with the best in your kitchen and see what wonders you can create.

Aromatics

The Veggie Trinity, often referred to as aromatics, is the first thing to go into any soup pot. Each culture has its own name for the combination. In France it is "mirepoix." Latino chefs refer to it as "sofrito." In Italy it is "soffrito."

This triad is the base for most soups and sauces and includes celery, carrot or green pepper, and onion. When these ingredients are sautéed and simmered, they combine to emit a luscious flavor and aroma that start our mouths watering.

Creating stock is much more of an art than a science. Knowing the starter ingredients makes the seemingly monumental task of making stock an easy exercise. The following recipes will give you an outline of what to use, but they are only suggestions. The amounts of each aromatic you use aren't precise.

Classically, a mirepoix is a mixture of 50 percent onion, 25 percent carrot, and 25 percent celery that enhances the flavor, aroma, and balance of stocks.

This combination of vegetables adds layers of flavor and depth to a stock. I frequently add garlic, mushrooms, and leeks. There should be approximately one pound of mirepoix or sofrito to one gallon of meat stock. If you're making vegetable stock, you should use four pounds of mirepoix or sofrito to one gallon of water, or one part vegetables to two parts of water.

Tasting your stock is key. Sample it at different stages, adding herbs and other seasonings and more aromatics, if necessary. Another shortcut I often use is to make up a large batch of mirepoix or sofrito. I reserve the portion I need for the recipe I'm creating, then I

divide the balance of the mirepoix or sofrito into half-cup portions in ziplock plastic bags, which I label, date, and freeze for up to six months. Whenever I want to make soup, all I need to do is thaw a bag and I'm off and running.

Another option is to pour the cooled mixture into clean ice cube trays and freeze. When the mixture is frozen, remove the cubes from the trays and save them in the freezer in a ziplock plastic freezer bag. I can then use the cubes as needed as a flavoring or base for my soups, sauces, and stews.

Whenever you see onion, carrots or green bell pepper, and celery listed in the recipes that follow, feel free to use an equal quantity of your choice of mirepoix, white mirepoix, sofrito, or soffrito, depending on what flavors you desire.

Traditional Mirepoix

Here is a simple recipe for mirepoix, based on the classic proportions of 1 part carrots and 1 part celery to 2 parts onion.
Yield: about 8 cups

1 T butter
1 T olive oil
4 c onion, chopped
2 c carrots, peeled and chopped
2 c celery, chopped

Melt the butter with the olive oil in a large stockpot. Add the vegetables and sauté over medium heat until the onion is translucent. Remove from the heat and refrigerate or freeze until you're ready to use it in soup.

White Mirepoix

A white stock is made by simmering bones, vegetables, and aromatics in water. The mirepoix for this stock remains almost colorless throughout the cooking process.
Yield: about 10 cups

1 T butter
1 T olive oil
2 c onion, chopped
2 c leeks, chopped
2 c celery, chopped
2 c parsnips, peeled and chopped
2 c very clean mushrooms or mushroom trimmings

Melt the butter with the olive oil in a large stockpot. Add the vegetables and sauté until the onion is translucent.

Add to your meats and stock as your recipe instructs, or refrigerate or freeze to use later.

Spanish Sofrito

Sofrito is a traditional base for many Latino and Spanish dishes, but adds wonderful flavor and depth to almost any meal. Annatto oil is available at many grocery stores.
Yield: about 6 cups

2 T annatto or olive oil
3 c finely chopped onion
1 c finely chopped green bell pepper
1 c finely chopped red bell pepper
1 jalapeño, chopped
5 cloves garlic, minced
1 T tomato paste
½ c chopped cilantro
¼ t salt

¼ t black pepper
1 lime, juice and zest

Heat the oil in a heavy skillet over medium-high heat. Add the onion and sauté 1 minute. Add the bell peppers, jalapeño, garlic, and tomato paste. Cook 10 minutes, stirring frequently.

Stir in the remaining ingredients. Use in your favorite soup or sauce, or freeze for later use.

Italian Soffrito

Soffrito means under- or lightly fried. Dozens of Italian dishes use soffrito as a base, especially for soups, stews, and sauces.
Yield: about 8 cups

¼ c olive oil
6 large onions, chopped
4 cloves garlic, minced
1 c chopped parsley
3 T chopped basil
1 c fresh (or dried and reconstituted)
   porcini mushrooms
2 c peeled and crushed tomatoes, or 1 2-lb can,
   with liquid
¼ t nutmeg
1 t salt
freshly ground black pepper, to taste

If you are using dried mushrooms, soak them in 2 cups of warm water for approximately 30 minutes. Reserve the soaking liquid.

Heat the oil in a large frying pan over medium heat. Stir in the onion and cook for 2 minutes, stirring frequently. Add the garlic and cook until the onion is soft. Add the parsley and basil, and cook until the parsley loses its intense green color. Add the mushrooms; if you are using dried mushrooms, strain the mushroom soaking water and add ¼ cup of the liquid to the pan. Add the tomatoes, nutmeg, salt, and pepper, and simmer over low heat until the liquid reduces by a quarter, about 30 minutes. Use immediately or freeze.

Stocks

The liquid in many soups comes from water that has been seasoned with the essence of meats, seafood, or vegetables. Here are some suggestions for making your own stock. I use the words "stock" and "broth" interchangeably in the recipes that follow, although broth is usually from a can and stock refers to the homemade variety. Add the vegetables that you prefer to create a soup your family will love. If you'd like to use mirepoix (see page 13), substitute it for the same quantity of vegetables in the recipe. Stock can be refrigerated for up to four days or stored in the freezer for up to six months.

Chicken or Turkey Stock

Yield: 3 quarts

4 lb chicken or turkey bones, cut into pieces
chicken or turkey giblets and neck, chopped
3 qt plus 1 c cold water
1 medium onion
2 leeks, halved lengthwise and rinsed
2 carrots
2 stalks celery, halved
2 t salt
6 sprigs parsley
6 sprigs fresh thyme
3 cloves garlic
3 bay leaves

In a kettle, combine the chicken or turkey bones, giblets, neck, and 3 quarts of cold water. Bring to a boil. Skim the foam from the top and discard.

Add another cup of cold water and bring to a boil again. Skim the foam from the top again and discard.

Add the onion, leeks, carrots, celery, salt, parsley, thyme, garlic, and bay leaves. Lower the heat and simmer the stock for 2 hours, continuing to skim and discard the foam as it forms.

Remove the chicken or turkey from the kettle. Let cool for 10 minutes or until it's cool enough to handle. Remove the meat and skin from the bones, and reserve the meat for later use.

Break apart the bones and return them with the skin to the kettle. Simmer the stock for 2 more hours, adding boiling water if necessary to keep the bones covered.

Strain the stock through a fine sieve into a bowl, pressing hard on the solids, and let it cool. Discard the solids and chill the stock. When the stock has cooled, remove the congealed fat on top with a slotted spoon.

Chicken Stock—Double-Day Doozie

This slow-cooked chicken stock has outstanding flavor. It's worth the extra day to prepare.
Yield: 3 quarts

Day One:

- 5 lb fresh chicken bones (necks, backs, wings)
- 5 qt cold water
- 2½ inches gingerroot, cut into ½-inch chunks
- 2 baby Vidalia onions or 2 bunches of scallions, cut into 1-inch chunks
- 2 c chopped celery
- 2 c chopped carrots
- 4 cloves garlic
- 1 large red onion, thinly sliced
- 10 white peppercorns
- 10 red or pink peppercorns

Day Two:

- 3 qt chicken stock, from Day One
- 2 qt cold water
- 5 lb fresh chicken bones (necks, backs, wings)
- 2½ inches gingerroot, cut into ½-inch chunks
- 2 baby Vidalia onions or 2 bunches of scallions, cut into 1-inch chunks
- 2 c chopped celery
- 2 c chopped carrots
- 4 cloves garlic
- 1 large red onion, thinly sliced
- 10 white peppercorns
- 10 red or pink peppercorns

Day One:

Rinse the chicken bones under cold running water. Place bones in a heavy 10-quart stockpot. Add the cold water and set the pot over high heat. Bring to a boil. Reduce the heat and simmer for 10 minutes, or until there is a thick foam on the surface. Skim off and discard the foam.

Add the remaining ingredients for Day One and simmer on low for 4 hours, or until the liquid is reduced by half. Strain the finished stock through several layers of cheesecloth and discard the solids. Chill overnight.

Day Two:

Skim off the congealed fat from Day One's stock with a slotted spoon. Repeat the process from Day One, starting with Day One's stock and using the ingredients for Day Two.

Brown Chicken Stock

The light flavor of pear enhances this hearty stock. Winterport Winery Dry Pear white wine works well in this recipe (see appendix).
Yield: 2 quarts

5 lb chicken bones
10 c water, or enough to cover the chicken by 2 inches
1 large onion, cut into 1-inch chunks
2 carrots, cut into 1-inch chunks
2 stalks celery, cut into 1-inch chunks
1 bay leaf
10 peppercorns
1 bunch parsley stems
1 c dry white wine

Preheat the oven to 450° F. Rinse the bones in cold water. Place them in a roasting pan and roast, stirring occasionally, until well browned all over.

Transfer the roasted bones to a stockpot. Cover with water and simmer for 30 minutes. Skim the foam off the top of the liquid carefully and discard.

While you are simmering the bones, place the vegetables in the same roasting pan used for the bones and roast them until they brown. Add the vegetables to the stockpot.

Place the hot roasting pan over medium heat on the stove top and pour in the wine.

Stir and scrape up all the browned bits stuck to the bottom and sides of the pan and pour everything into the stockpot. Add the bay leaf, peppercorns, and parsley. Continue to simmer on low, uncovered, for 4 hours.

Strain the stock through a fine sieve into a bowl, pressing hard on the solids, and let the stock cool. Discard the solids and chill the stock. When the stock has cooled, scrape off the congealed fat with a slotted spoon.

Note: If you want to clarify the stock, whisk 4 egg whites in a bowl and add them to the stock in your stockpot. Stir gently and constantly to prevent the whites from sticking to the bottom and sides of the pot. Bring the stock to a boil. The egg whites will rise to the top. Once they have risen, stop stirring.

The whites will solidify on the top of the liquid, forming a soft crust, and any impurities and fats will cling to it. Carefully skim the egg layer off the top and discard. The stock liquid will be transparent.

Hearty Beef Stock

This is a full-flavored stock for your favorite beef stew. I ask my butcher for his freshest and meatiest bones for my stock.
Yield: 4 quarts

4 lb beef bones
4 qt cold water
2 c chopped carrots
2 c chopped white onion
2 c chopped celery
2 leeks, washed well and chopped
6 garlic cloves, crushed
2 bay leaves
1 small bunch parsley
4 sprigs fresh thyme
1 sprig fresh rosemary
10 black peppercorns

Place the bones in a large stockpot and cover with the water. Bring to a boil. Reduce the heat and simmer 10 minutes.

Skim the fat and foam from the surface and discard both. Add the remaining ingredients. Partially cover the pot, and allow the mixture to simmer for 3 hours. Add water if necessary during the cooking process to keep the bones covered.

Strain through a fine-mesh sieve and discard the solids. Cool and refrigerate.

White Veal Stock

This stock is an elegant beginning for beef stew, soups, and gravies.
Yield: 4 quarts

4 lb veal bones
4 qt cold water
2 c chopped carrots
1 c chopped white onion
1 c chopped celery
2 leeks, washed well and chopped
4 garlic cloves, crushed
1 bay leaf
1 small bunch parsley
4 sprigs fresh thyme

Place the bones in a large stockpot and cover with the water. Bring to a boil. Reduce the heat and simmer. Skim the fat and foam from the surface and discard them. Add the remaining ingredients. Partially cover the pot and allow the mixture to simmer for 3 hours. Add water if necessary during the cooking process to keep the bones covered. Strain through a fine mesh sieve and discard the solids. Cool and refrigerate.

Two Seafood Stocks

After a lobster feed, in true Maine tradition, we use all the lobster shells and bodies to make a delicious stock. Winterport Winery's Dry Pear white wine is excellent in a lobster or shrimp stock. Fish stock enhances the flavor of chowders and bouillabaisse.

Lobster or Shrimp Stock
Yield: 2 quarts

5 lb Maine lobster shells and/or bodies or Maine shrimp heads and shells
10 c water
1 c coarsely chopped carrots
1 c coarsely chopped celery
1 c peeled and coarsely chopped leeks
2 bay leaves
5 sprigs parsley
10 peppercorns
1 c dry white wine

Place all the ingredients in a large, heavy stockpot and bring to a boil. Reduce the heat and simmer gently for 30 minutes.

Remove the stock from the heat; strain the mixture through a fine mesh strainer and discard the solids.

Return the liquid to the stove top and simmer over moderate heat until it is reduced to about 2 quarts.

Fish Stock
Yield: 4 quarts

6 lb fish bones, heads, fins, or fillets
2 T olive oil
1 c chopped onion
1 c sliced leek, white part only
1 c chopped celery
1 c chopped carrot
1 c chopped cremini mushrooms
2 c white wine (optional)
1 bay leaf
3 sprigs sage
3 sprigs thyme
3 sprigs parsley
1 t freshly ground white pepper
4 qt cold water

Rinse fish parts under running water for at least 5 minutes. Drain them in a colander. If you are using the heads, remove the eyes.

Heat oil in a large saucepan and cook vegetables on low for 6 minutes. Add fish parts and cook for 5 minutes. Pour in the wine, cook for 5 minutes, and add remaining ingredients. Cover vegetables and fish completely with water, adding more if necessary. Bring to a boil, then reduce heat and simmer for 30 minutes. Skim as necessary to remove foam. Remove stock from heat and let it stand for 30 minutes. Skim once more. Strain stock through a fine-mesh strainer and discard solids. Refrigerate stock overnight.

Remove the fat layer on top and discard. Absorb remaining fat with a paper towel.

Slow-Cooker Vegetable Stock

When creating a flavorful veggie stock, I've found it best to use at least one part vegetables to two parts liquid. That means if you are using 12 cups of water, you need a good 6 cups of vegetables to flavor the liquid. This recipe uses an even richer one-to-one ratio for maximum flavor in a slow cooker.
Yield: 6 cups

V10 Vegetables

Veggies are the champions of our culinary world. They make every savory soup taste better. My Top Ten vegetables for soups and stews are:

1. Onion
2. Carrot
3. Celery
4. Leek
5. Squash
6. Parsnip
7. Potato, both white and sweet
8. Mushrooms
9. Peas
10. Beans

2 c chopped onion
1 c chopped carrots
1 c chopped celery
1 c chopped parsnip
1 c chopped button mushrooms
3 cloves garlic, sliced in half
3 bay leaves

2 sprigs thyme
6 c cold water

Combine all ingredients in a slow cooker. Cook over low heat for 6 to 8 hours. Strain and discard the solids.

Vegan "Chicken" Stock

Here is another tasty adaptation for vegetarians. Unlike most stocks, it is cooked for only a brief time.
Yield: 1 quart

1 c chopped carrots
1 c chopped celery
1 c chopped shiitake mushrooms
4 c water
2 bay leaves
½ t celery seeds
1 t rubbed sage
½ t salt
3 sprigs parsley
3 T nutritional yeast

Combine all ingredients in a large stockpot. Bring to a boil and simmer for 15 minutes.

Strain the stock through a fine-mesh sieve. Pick out the vegetables from the herbs and save them for soup or casseroles, as they have not been cooked to death. Discard the herbs.

CLEAR SOUPS

Simple, clear broths can contain a myriad of complex flavors. Embrace your inner culinary artist and try your hand at one of these delicious clear soups. Their beauty lies in their simplicity.

Maine French Onion Soup with Canadian Bacon

French onion soup is wonderful topped with slivers of Canadian bacon, shredded cheese, and artisanal bread. When you use crusty slices of Borealis Bread and State of Maine Cheese Company's Saint Croix Black Pepper Jack cheese (see appendix), you've got a doubly delicious combination.

Serves 6

3 T butter
1 T olive oil
6 medium onions, sliced in half then thinly sliced
2 T fresh minced garlic
3 T Maine maple syrup
1 c marsala wine
½ t freshly ground white pepper
3 c chicken stock
3 c canned beef broth
1 T chicken bouillon paste or powder
1 T beef bouillon paste or powder
12 slices Canadian bacon, cut into slivers
   or chopped
8 slices artisanal bread, toasted
1 c grated Gruyère cheese (or more)
½ c grated Parmesan (or more)
½ c grated black pepper Jack cheese (or more)

In a large, heavy-bottomed saucepan, melt the butter over medium heat. Add the oil, onion, garlic, and maple syrup. Cook, stirring often, for 20 to 25 minutes, or until the onion is caramel brown.

Deglaze the pan: Add the marsala and scrape up all the tasty brown bits from the bottom of the pan. Add the pepper, stock, broth, and chicken and beef bouillon. Reduce the heat and simmer, covered, for 30 minutes.

Preheat the broiler. Taste and adjust seasonings. Ladle soup into oven-proof bowls. Top each bowl with a layer of Canadian bacon, a slice of toast, and the grated cheeses. Broil until the cheeses melt and bubble.

Quick Chicken Noodle Soup

Always a crowd pleaser, this soup has been my daughter Elizabeth's favorite since she was a baby.
Serves 4 to 6

1 T butter
½ c chopped onion
½ c chopped celery
1 c sliced carrots
6 c chicken broth
2 c chopped cooked chicken breast
1 T chicken bouillon paste or powder
1½ c egg noodles or alphabet pasta
salt and pepper, to taste
1 T chopped fresh parsley

In a large saucepan, melt butter over medium heat. Cook the onion, celery, and carrots in the butter until they are fork-tender, about 5 minutes. Pour in the chicken broth and stir in the chicken, bouillon, and noodles. Add salt and pepper and bring to a boil. Reduce heat and simmer 20 minutes.

Adjust the seasonings and serve sprinkled with fresh parsley.

Beef Vegetable Soup

So easy and so good. Add any other fresh herbs you like to vary the flavor.
Serves 6

1½ lb ground sirloin
6 c beef broth
3 T minced garlic
1 c diced white onion
2 c sliced carrots
2 c diced celery
2 c sliced Maine potatoes
1 c cut green beans, drained if canned
2 c corn, drained if canned
2 c tomato sauce
1 c diced tomatoes, drained if canned
1 t ground mustard
½ t freshly ground white pepper

Maine sea salt, to taste
red pepper flakes, to taste

In a large saucepan, brown the ground sirloin and break it into small pieces. Remove the meat with a slotted spoon and drain it on a paper-towel–lined plate. Reserve 1 tablespoon of the fat in the pan and discard the rest. Add all of the remaining ingredients to the pan. Stir to combine and bring to a boil, stirring occasionally. Reduce heat and return the beef to the soup. Cover and simmer 2 hours. Add additional beef broth if you wish to thin the soup.

Turkey Soup for a Crowd

This is the quintessential post-Thanksgiving delight. Make the stock using the turkey bones from your feast. If you have leftover stuffing, you can heat it up and float a spoonful on top of each bowl of soup just before serving. Mashed potato is an excellent addition—just substitute it for the chopped potatoes and add it with the stock. Almost any leftover vegetables can go in the pot. A side of cranberry sauce is a delicious accompaniment.

Serves 10

1 T butter
1 c chopped onion
1 c chopped celery
1 c sliced carrots
2 c chopped potatoes
8 c turkey stock
2 T turkey bouillon paste or powder
4 c chopped cooked turkey, both white and dark meat
1 c corn
1 c sweet baby peas
1 t sage
1 t thyme

salt and pepper, to taste
3 T chopped fresh parsley, for garnish

In a large saucepan, melt the butter over medium heat. Cook the onion, celery, carrots, and potatoes in butter until fork tender, about 5 minutes.

Pour in the turkey stock, and stir in the bouillon, turkey, corn, and peas. Bring to a boil. Reduce the heat and simmer 20 minutes.

Add the sage, thyme, salt, and pepper. Adjust seasonings to your liking. Serve sprinkled with fresh parsley.

Chicken Margarita Soup with Red Onion Guacamole

If you like the flavors of cilantro and spicy peppers with a touch of tequila, you'll love this concoction. Serve this soup with a side of guacamole, a dollop of sour cream, and a handful of tortilla chips.
Serves 4 to 6

6 c chicken stock
4 limes, zest and juice
3 serrano peppers, seeded and finely chopped
2 Anaheim peppers, seeded and finely chopped
8 scallions, thinly sliced
2 cloves garlic, minced
1 t cumin
½ c chopped cilantro
4 c cooked chicken, cut in bite-sized pieces
1 oz tequila
thin wedges of lime and salt, for garnish
tortilla chips

Pour chicken stock in a medium saucepan. Add the lime zest, peppers, half of the scallions, and garlic. Simmer, covered, 20 minutes.

Pour the soup through a fine mesh strainer and discard the solids. Add the cumin, cilantro, and chicken. Heat through. Add the lime juice and tequila and serve or, for an exciting variation, rub the rims of the soup bowls with a wedge of lime and dip in salt. Wait to add the tequila until you have the individual bowls dished up, then pour a splash of tequila on top of each.

Garnish with lime wedges. Serve with tortilla chips and Red Onion Guacamole.

Red Onion Guacamole:
2 ripe avocados, chopped
1 small vine-ripened tomato
1 c finely minced red onion
1 fresh serrano pepper, with seeds and
    membranes removed and minced
2 T chopped cilantro
1 T fresh lime juice
1 t tequila (optional)
1 t Maine sea salt
½ t coarsely ground black pepper
cayenne pepper, to taste

Place all ingredients in a medium bowl. Mix well and season to taste with cayenne pepper.

Fiddlehead Soup

Fiddlehead ferns are one of Maine's delightful indications that winter has ended. Their season is short, so eat them while you can.
Serves 4

2 lb Maine fiddleheads (fresh asparagus may be substituted)
3 T unsalted butter
1 large Vidalia onion, chopped
2 ribs celery, chopped
2 garlic cloves, crushed
4 c vegetable stock
1 T vegetable bouillon paste or powder
1 T chopped fresh basil
1 T chopped fresh oregano
1 T chopped fresh parsley
Maine sea salt and freshly ground black pepper, to taste

Place fiddleheads in a large bowl, cover with cold water, and drain. Trim any brown ends. Be sure they are cleaned well. Reserve 12 or so small pretty ones for garnish and coarsely chop the rest.

In a large saucepan, melt the butter over medium heat. Add the onion and cook until translucent. Add the fiddleheads, toss to coat them with butter, and cook 2 minutes. Add the remaining ingredients, bring to a simmer, and cook 15 minutes.

Float the reserved fiddleheads in the hot soup and let them blanch. Remove the fiddleheads from the pan and set aside. Dish up the soup and top with the blanched fiddleheads.

Dandelion Soup

Gather your greens early in the season while they are tender, harvesting only from unsprayed areas.
Serves 4

½ lb dandelion greens (or chickory leaves)
1 T Maine sea salt
2 T extra-virgin olive oil
1 T chicken or vegetable bouillon paste or powder
1 c chopped tomato
4 c chicken stock

Rinse the greens in a large bowl of cold water, swishing them gently to let any grit fall to the bottom. Lift the greens from the water, leaving any grit behind. Chop them into bite-sized pieces.

Fill a large saucepan with water, stir in the salt, and bring to a full boil. Add the greens and blanch for 3 minutes to remove bitterness.

In another saucepan, heat the olive oil over medium heat. Transfer the blanched greens to the saucepan and sauté, stirring constantly. Add the bouillon and tomato and sauté 2 more minutes. Add the chicken stock, bring to a simmer, and cook for 10 minutes. Serve with small crackers.

Asian Chicken Pepper Pot with Chili-Chive Oil

If you are looking for a spicy version of wonton soup, here it is. If you cannot find thick sweet soy sauce, you can substitute molasses. Both wonton wrappers and edammame are readily available in either the produce or freezer section of most supermarkets.
Serves 6

2 lemons, zest and juice
6 c chicken stock
1-inch piece gingerroot, grated
10 Szechwan peppercorns
3 Anaheim peppers, seeded and finely chopped
8 scallions, thinly sliced
2 cloves garlic, minced
1 T soy sauce
1 to 2 t thick sweet soy sauce or molasses, to taste
1 stalk lemongrass
4 oz wonton wrappers
¼ c chopped cilantro
4 c cooked chicken, cut in bite-sized pieces
2 c edammame (green soybeans)
black sesame seeds, for garnish

Cut zest off the lemons in wide strips, being sure to remove only the yellow layer and not the entire peel. Pour the chicken stock in a medium saucepan and add the ginger, lemon zest, peppercorns, peppers, half of the scallions, garlic, soy sauce, and sweet soy sauce.

Peel any dry outer leaves off the lemongrass. Crush the lemongrass with the side of a chef's knife or bend it back and forth a few times to release the oils. Cut into 2-inch sections and add them to the pan. Simmer 30 minutes.

Pour soup through a fine mesh strainer into a saucepan and discard the solids. Cut the wonton wrappers into ¾-inch strips.

Add the cilantro, chicken, edammame, and wonton wrapper strips to the soup. Simmer gently for 15 minutes.

Serve sprinkled with sesame seeds and the remaining scallions. Drizzle with Chili-Chive Oil.

Chili-Chive Oil:
¼ c extra-virgin olive oil
¼ c coarsely chopped chives
½ t cayenne pepper

Purée the oil, chives, and cayenne in a blender. Pour through a fine mesh strainer. It's handy to use a squirt bottle to dispense this oil.

Hot and Sour Soup

Traditionally served in Asian restaurants, this spicy, tangy soup is great for easing the symptoms of a cold. Winterport Winery Apple wine (see appendix) adds remarkable flavor to this recipe.
Serves 4 to 6

2 t sesame oil
1 T sambal oelek (chili paste; see next page)
1 T grated gingerroot
1 T finely sliced lemongrass
4 garlic cloves, minced
4 c chicken stock
1 T beef bouillon paste or powder
1 c coarsely chopped wood ear mushrooms or wild mushrooms of your choice
2 c dry white wine
2 T lime juice
5 T soy sauce
2 T thick sweet soy sauce (substitute molasses if you can't find sweet soy sauce)
1 t fish sauce

4 T white vinegar
2 eggs, lightly beaten
2 T coarsely chopped pickled ginger
4 c coarsely chopped baby spinach
1 red bell pepper, thinly sliced
½ lb cooked chicken breast or pork tenderloin, cut into bite-sized pieces
1 lb silken tofu, cut into ½-inch cubes
1 t freshly ground white pepper
2 T cornstarch, mixed with 3 T cold water
scallions, thinly sliced, for garnish (optional)

In a large saucepan, heat sesame oil over low heat and cook the sambal oelek, ginger, lemongrass, and garlic until their aromas release. Add the chicken stock and bouillon and simmer, covered, 20 minutes.

Add the mushrooms, wine, lime juice, both soy sauces, fish sauce, and vinegar. Bring to a simmer. Stirring constantly, add the eggs. Continue stirring until the eggs cook and are distributed throughout the soup. Add the pickled ginger, spinach, red pepper, chicken or pork, tofu, and white pepper. Stir in the cornstarch mixture. Simmer 10 minutes, stirring occasionally, until thickened.

Adjust seasoning with additional sambal oelek and white pepper to create the heat you desire.

Serve topped with a sprinkle of sliced scallions.

Note: If you can't find Sambal Oelek in your local market, it's simple to make at home.

Sambal Oelek:
Yield: 1 cup
   12 medium red chili peppers, seeded
      and chopped
   2 t salt

Puree in a food processor. Keep refrigerated.

Vegetable Soup

All-you-can-eat vegetable soup. With its low calorie count, this soup is freedom in a bowl. It's wonderful when eating healthfully tastes so good! This recipe makes a large batch, but it freezes well. For a nourishing vegetarian meal, choose vegetable bouillon paste or powder and stock, and serve with a lightly dressed salad.
Serves 4 to 6

2 T olive oil
3 large onions, chopped
6 carrots, peeled and chopped
6 ribs celery, chopped
3 cloves garlic, minced
1 28-oz can diced tomatoes, with juice
3 c cauliflower florets
2 c cut fresh yellow wax beans
3 zucchini, chopped
6 c fresh baby spinach
2 c chopped fresh kale
¼ c chopped fresh basil
½ c chopped fresh parsley

2 T chicken or vegetable bouillon paste or powder
½ t freshly ground black pepper
12 c chicken or vegetable stock
snipped chives or chopped celery leaves,
   for garnish

In a large saucepan, heat the oil over medium heat. Add the onion, carrots, celery, and garlic. Cook, stirring occasionally, 5 minutes. Add remaining ingredients and bring to a boil. Reduce the heat to low and simmer, covered, for 30 minutes. Adjust the balance of salt and pepper. Garnish with chives or celery leaves.

Maine Seafood Stew with Fresh Tuna and Macadamia Nuts

Sweet and savory combine for a delectable, rich soup. The fresh tuna is a surprise, and the myriad textures dance across your tongue.
Serves 6

2 T olive oil
2 c chopped onion
2-inch piece gingerroot, peeled and grated
3 cloves garlic, minced
2 jalapeños, seeded and finely chopped
2 c chopped vine-ripened tomatoes
2 T fresh lime juice
4 T paprika
⅔ c coconut milk
2 c fish stock
1 T chicken bouillon paste or powder
½ lb Maine shrimp, peeled
½ lb Maine scallops
½ c finely chopped cilantro leaves
salt to taste
1 t black pepper
½ lb sushi-grade (extremely fresh) tuna
½ c finely chopped macadamia nuts, for garnish

In a large saucepan, heat the oil in a large pan over low heat. Add the onion and cook for 15 minutes.

Stir in the ginger, garlic, jalapeños, and 1 cup of the tomatoes. Cook 5 minutes. Add the lime juice and paprika. Cook for 2 minutes. Add coconut milk, stock, and bouillon. Bring the mixture to a simmer. Add the remaining tomatoes, shrimp, and scallops. Return the soup to a simmer and cook for 5 minutes. Add the cilantro, reserving 2 tablespoons for garnish, and adjust the balance of salt and pepper.

Cut the tuna across the grain into thin slices; cut the slices into very thin strips and divide them into six portions.

To serve, place a portion of fresh tuna in each of six bowls and ladle a generous amount of the hot soup on top of the tuna. To serve, sprinkle the soup with the reserved cilantro and the macadamia nuts.

CREAMY SOUPS

Warm and creamy soups are the ultimate comfort food for me. Steaming potato soup, luscious butternut squash bisque, warm and hearty tomato soup with fresh herbs—all are on the menu when I want to feel close to home. Whether smooth or chunky, creamy soups will always satisfy your deepest hunger.

Maine Lobster Stew

Whether you call it stew or bisque, this soup is pure gold—just the flavors of lobster, butter, and cream.

Serves 4

4 c cold water
1½-lb Maine lobster, cooked and shelled
4 T unsalted butter
4 c light cream
1 c lobster stock
½ t salt

Heat the cold water in a large, covered pot. When the water comes to a boil, add the lobster and steam it for 12 to 15 minutes. Remove the lobster from the pot and let it drain in a colander.

If you don't have any lobster stock, strain the steaming liquid from the pot through a fine-mesh sieve lined with cheesecloth, reserving 2 cups.

Shuck the lobster. Cut the tail, knuckle, and claw meat into bite-sized pieces.

Melt the butter in a deep skillet or heavy saucepan and add the lobster meat. Sauté 2 minutes on low heat. Add the cream and lobster stock or reserved steaming water, and bring the ingredients just barely to a bubble. Simmer on low heat 15 minutes, stirring occasionally.

Serve hot with a slice or two of crusty bread per serving.

Damariscotta Oyster Bisque

People travel across the globe for Damariscotta River oysters. The Pemaquid Oyster Festival held every fall serves up dishes of all sorts, but this one is a crowd favorite.
Serves 4

1 qt Maine oysters, shucked
2 c cold water
2 T finely chopped onion
2 T flour mixed with 2 T cold water
2½ c milk or light cream
2 T butter
1 t paprika
salt and pepper, to taste
dash of Tabasco (optional)

Drain the oysters in a colander, saving the nectar. Rinse the oysters thoroughly and place them in a saucepan. Add the reserved nectar, water, and onion. Boil 3 to 5 minutes. Remove the oysters, saving the broth in the pan.

When the oysters are cool enough to handle, cut them into small pieces and return them to the pan with the broth. Thicken the broth with the flour and water mixture. Bring to a boil. Add the milk or cream and butter. Season to taste with paprika, salt, and pepper, and add a dash of Tabasco, if desired.

Serve hot with saltines or oyster crackers.

Acorn Squash Soup with Kale

Creamy and golden with a smattering of green, this soup is delicious with fresh greens and a slice of focaccia alongside.
Serves 4 to 6

4 c turkey or chicken stock
2 large Vidalia onions, diced
3 c acorn squash, cut in bite-size pieces
1 t Maine sea salt
1 t white pepper, or to taste
2 c finely chopped kale
3 T Maine maple syrup
1 c heavy cream or soy milk

Garnish:
  2 T heavy cream
  ½ c freshly grated Parmigiano-Reggiano cheese
  snipped chives or sliced scallions

Place stock, onion, and squash in a large, heavy-bottomed pot. Bring to a boil. Lower the heat and simmer, covered, for 30 minutes.

Season with salt and pepper and add the kale. Simmer another 5 minutes, until the kale is completely cooked through but hasn't lost all its color. Add the maple syrup and heavy cream. No more boiling now. Just let the cream come up to temperature over very low heat. Taste and adjust seasonings to your liking.

Serve with a drizzle of heavy cream, a sprinkle of cheese, and a few chive or scallion bits for color.

Tomato Bisque with Fresh Basil Ribbons

This simple, creamy soup is enhanced by the bright flavor of fresh basil. It's delicious either warm or at room temperature, by the bowl or atop pasta with steamed broccoli, carrots, and a touch of garlic oil for a complete meal. For an elegant touch, top the soup with fresh baby spinach leaves and lobster-tail medallions.

Serves 4 generously

3 T olive oil
1 T unsalted butter or olive oil
1 large Vidalia or other sweet onion, minced
3 cloves garlic, minced
¼ c dry sherry
1 28-oz can chopped tomatoes or 6 large tomatoes, peeled, seeded, and chopped
1 t salt
1 t white or black pepper
2 T sugar
12 large basil leaves
1 c light cream or soy milk

Heat the olive oil and butter in a medium saucepan over medium heat. Add the onion and garlic and sauté until the onion is transparent. Stir often—do not let the onion or garlic brown.

Deglaze the pan with sherry: Add the sherry to the onion and stir well, scraping the bottom to incorporate all of the bits of flavor. Cook the sherry and onion on medium-low heat for 10 minutes. Add the tomatoes and cook over low heat another 10 minutes, stirring often. Season with the salt, pepper, and sugar.

Wash the basil leaves well and pat dry with

paper towels. Stack the leaves one on top of the other on a cutting board. Roll the leaves up into a tight cylinder, with the stems at the bottom and the tips at the top. Using a sharp knife and starting at the tips, carefully cut the leaves into ⅛-inch slices. End just before the stems. (Save the stems in a zip-lock bag in the freezer for the next time you want extra flavor in your homemade stock.) Lift the basil ribbons gently and sprinkle them down on the cutting board to unfurl and separate them. This is called a chiffonade of basil.

Now is the time to blend your soup—you should leave some chunks for texture. If you have an immersion blender, it is perfect for blending the soup right in the pan. If you use a regular blender, process the soup briefly by the cupful, being careful not to burn yourself, and return all of the processed soup to the pan.

When all the tomatoes and onion are coarsely blended, add the cream or soy milk to the pan and stir. Heat the soup on low just until it's warm enough for your taste.

Ladle the soup into bowls and sprinkle with the basil ribbons. You are ready to eat!

Five Mushroom Soup

Winterport Winery (see appendix) makes a delicous blueberry wine that's perfect for this recipe.
Serves 8

3 T unsalted butter, softened
½ c minced shallots
1 c coarsely chopped cremini mushrooms
1 c coarsely chopped oyster mushrooms
1 c coarsely chopped maitake or matsutake mushrooms
1 c coarsely chopped portobello mushrooms
1 c coarsely chopped shiitake mushrooms
1 T chicken or vegetable bouillon paste or powder
1 T minced fresh sage or tarragon
3 T minced garlic
8 c chicken stock
1 lb Maine potatoes, cut into bite-sized chunks
¼ c Maine blueberry wine
½ t salt
½ t pepper
¼ t cayenne pepper
½ c snipped fresh chives

1 c heavy cream
½ c finely chopped fresh flat leaf parsley

Melt the butter in a large, heavy saucepan over medium-high heat. Add the shallots and sauté 3 minutes. Add all of the mushrooms and the bouillon. Sauté 5 minutes. Add the sage or tarragon and garlic and cook 10 more minutes. Stir in the chicken stock and potatoes and bring to a boil. Reduce the heat, cover, and simmer for 30 minutes.

With a potato masher, gently press the solids and "mash" the potatoes in the soup. Stir well after mashing, being sure to scrape up and incorporate all of the bits from the bottom of the pan. Add the wine, salt, peppers, and 3 tablespoons of the snipped chives. Heat to a simmer.

Stir in the heavy cream. Sprinkle with parsley and the remaining chives and serve.

Cauliflower and Mushroom Soup with Seared Scallops and Tobiko

The flavors of mushrooms and cauliflower are the perfect canvas for the seared scallops and beautiful orange tobiko, which is the roe of the flying fish. Tobiko is available in gourmet shops or through sushi restaurants (or you can substitute a favorite caviar). *Serves 6 to 8*

2 T olive oil
1 c chopped sweet onion
1 T minced garlic
2 c peeled and chopped turnip
2 portobello mushrooms, coarsely chopped
1 c chopped cremini mushrooms
5 c cauliflower florets (about 1 large head)
2 c water
4 c vegetable or chicken broth
2 T vegetable or chicken bouillon paste or powder
sea salt, to taste

freshly ground white pepper, to taste
2 c heavy cream
1 T butter
1 t olive oil
8 large sea scallops, rinsed and patted dry
2 T Maine maple syrup

Garnish:
 1 1-oz jar tobiko
 8 t Maine maple syrup
 snipped chives (optional)

Heat the oil in a heavy, large saucepan over medium heat. Add the onion and garlic. Sauté until the onion is translucent, about 5 minutes. Add the turnip and cook another 5 minutes. Add all of the mushrooms and cook 5 more minutes. Add the cauliflower, water, chicken broth, and bouillon, and bring the soup to boil. Reduce heat to low, cover, and simmer gently until the cauliflower is tender, about 20 minutes.

Use an immersion blender to purée the soup in the pan, or purée it in small batches in a blender and return the soup to the saucepan. Season with sea salt and white pepper. Add the cream and stir.

Remove the thin, tough muscle from the sides of the scallops. Sprinkle the scallops with salt and pepper.

Heat the butter and 1 teaspoon of olive oil in a medium skillet over high heat. Sear the scallops in the skillet until they are browned and just opaque in the center, about 1½ minutes per side. Drizzle them with 2 tablespoons of maple syrup in the pan; turn the scallops to coat both sides.

Ladle the soup into bowls. Place 1 scallop in each bowl; top scallops with tobiko. Drizzle with a scant teaspoon of maple syrup and sprinkle with chives.

Creamy Chicken Vegetable Soup

This soup is a weeknight favorite. Easy and fast from start to table.
Serves 4

2 T butter
2 c chopped chicken meat
1 c diced potatoes
1 c chopped onion
¼ c diced carrots
1 c chopped celery
1 T chopped green bell peppers
1 T minced garlic
6 c chicken broth
2 T chicken bouillon paste or powder
½ t thyme
½ t oregano
½ t sage
½ t crushed red pepper
½ c light cream

In a medium saucepan, melt the butter over medium heat and sauté the chicken until the meat is opaque. Add the potatoes, onion, carrots, celery, green pepper, and garlic. Cook over medium heat until the vegetables are crisp tender. Add broth, bouillon, thyme, oregano, sage, and red pepper. Bring to a boil. Cover and simmer 20 minutes.

Remove the soup from the heat. Stir in the cream, and you're ready to serve.

Chicken Apple Soup with Brie Toasts

The flavors of apples and chicken mingle in this light but hearty soup.
Serves 6

6 T butter
3 large Red Delicious apples, peeled and chopped
3 large Granny Smith apples, peeled and chopped
1 c chopped Vidalia onion
2 T minced garlic
5 c chicken broth
2 c heavy cream
3 c chopped cooked chicken
salt and pepper
1 Red Delicious and 1 Granny Smith apple, unpeeled and cut into 6 slices each
2 T fresh lemon juice
1 T Maine maple syrup
2 T snipped chives, for garnish

Melt 4 tablespoons of the butter in a large saucepan. Add the chopped apples, onion, and garlic. Cook 5 minutes. Add the chicken broth and simmer until the apples are tender, about 30 minutes.

Use an immersion blender to purée the soup in the pot, or purée it in small batches in a blender. Return the soup to the saucepan. Add the cream and chicken, stir well, and simmer 5 minutes. Season to taste with salt and pepper.

Mix the apple slices with lemon juice. Melt the remaining 2 tablespoons of butter in the skillet over medium heat. Add the apples and maple syrup and sauté until the apples are golden brown.

Ladle the soup into bowls. Top each bowl with 2 apple slices and sprinkle with chopped chives. Serve with Brie Toasts.

Brie Toasts:

6 thick slices crusty baguette, cut at an angle
¼ c olive oil
3 T minced garlic
2 T fresh chopped parsley
salt and pepper
6 slices Brie, each large enough to cover center of baguette slice

Preheat oven to 350 degrees F. In a small bowl, combine the oil, garlic, and parsley. Mix well. Spread one side of the baguette slices with a generous amount of the garlic mixture. Sprinkle with salt and pepper. Arrange the slices on a baking sheet, garlic side up. Place a slice of Brie on top of each slice of bread. Put in the oven and bake until golden, about 10 minutes.

Butternut Squash Bisque

This soup is golden and slightly sweet—delicious with a slice of Blue Cheese Apple Butter Puff (page 99).
Serves 4 to 6

4 c turkey or chicken stock
2 T turkey or chicken bouillon paste or powder
2 large Vidalia onions, minced
4 c cubed butternut squash
1 t sea salt
pinch cayenne
½ t cinnamon
¼ t nutmeg
1 t white pepper, to taste
3 T Maine maple syrup
1 c heavy cream or plain full-fat soy milk

Garnish:
2 T heavy cream
ground cinnamon or cinnamon sticks
3 T chopped parsley

Place stock, bouillon, onion, and squash in a large, heavy-bottomed pot. Bring to a boil, cover, and simmer for 30 minutes.

Season with salt, cayenne, cinnamon, nutmeg, and pepper. Add the syrup and cream or soy milk. Bring up to temperature over very low heat—do not boil. Adjust seasonings to your liking.

Serve with a drizzle of heavy cream, a sprinkle of cinnamon, and parsley for color.

Pear Bisque

Pear Bisque makes an elegant first course. Preferred wine is the Demi-Pear from Winterport Winery (see appendix).
Serves 6

3 T unsalted butter
½ c minced onion
1 small turnip, peeled and finely diced
1 T freshly grated ginger
2 T finely minced crystallized ginger
4 c chicken or vegetable stock
2½ lb firm but ripe pears, peeled and cut into
   ½-inch cubes
¼ lb dried pears, coarsely chopped
1½ c heavy cream
⅓ c pear wine
2 T fresh lemon juice
1 T lemon zest
3 T Maine maple syrup
½ t nutmeg
⅛ t allspice
⅛ t freshly ground white pepper, or to taste

Garnish (optional):
   ¼ c finely chopped pecans
   6 ½-inch slices from a log of chèvre

Melt the butter in a heavy saucepan over medium heat. Sauté the onion and turnip about 8 minutes or until tender, stirring frequently.

Stir in the fresh and crystallized ginger and sauté another 2 minutes. Pour in the stock and bring the ingredients to a boil. Add fresh and dried pears. Reduce heat to medium low and simmer 35 to 40 minutes, stirring occasionally.

Remove the pan from the heat. Use an immersion blender or food processor to purée the soup until smooth. Return the mixture to low heat, stir in the remaining ingredients, and season to taste. Simmer about 30 minutes, stirring often.

Serve in pretty bowls, with a slice of chèvre and a sprinkle of chopped pecans.

Herb Roasted Sugar Pumpkin Soup with Chèvre

In the fall when the sugar pumpkins are fresh off the vine, this soup engages you in the enchantment of the season. Excellent chèvre can be ordered from Appleton Creamery (see appendix)
Serves 8

2-lb sugar pumpkin, peeled, seeded, and cut
   into 1-inch chunks
1 T chopped fresh sage
1 T chopped fresh rosemary
1 T Maine maple syrup
2 T Maine sea salt
½ t freshly ground black pepper
2 T melted butter
½ c chopped red onion
3 T coarsely chopped garlic
5 c chicken stock
1 c heavy cream
10 leaves sage, finely chopped
4 T chopped fresh rosemary
salt and white pepper
8 oz Maine chèvre (goat cheese)
cracked black pepper, for garnish

Preheat oven to 300 degrees F. Toss together the pumpkin, 1 tablespoon of sage, 1 tablespoon of rosemary, maple syrup, sea salt, pepper, butter, onion, and garlic in a heavy roasting pan and roast for 30 minutes.

Place the roasted vegetables and herbs in a large saucepan. Add 3 cups of the chicken stock and simmer 30 minutes, or until pumpkin is tender.

Use an immersion blender to purée the soup in the pot, or purée it in small batches in a blender. Return the soup to the saucepan. Add the cream, the rest of the sage and rosemary, salt and white pepper to taste, and enough of the remaining chicken stock to create the consistency you like. Spoon the chèvre into the soup. Stir until it is melted but not completely blended.

Dish up the soup and garnish with freshly cracked black pepper. Serve with a thick slice of warm bread.

For fun, serve this soup in little pumpkins. You'll need one small pumpkin per serving.

Preheat oven to 350 degrees F. Cut off the top of each pumpkin evenly and remove the seeds and stringy pulp. Scrape the inner walls until they are smooth. Trim the bottoms, if necessary, so the pumpkins don't wobble on the plates. Lightly season the insides of the pumpkins with salt and pepper. Bake for about 15 minutes; the pumpkin bowls should be warm but not completely cooked.

Remove pumpkins from oven. Set each pumpkin on a plate and ladle in the hot soup. For a more dramatic effect, place the tops back on before serving.

Thai Portobello Tortellini Bisque

East meets West in this spicy, creamy, full-flavored soup. Portobello mushrooms and crabmeat are my favored tortellini fillings, but if you have a different one you love, use it in this soup.

Serves 4

1 shallot, finely chopped
1 jalapeño pepper, seeded and finely chopped
2 t curry powder
2 T minced garlic
1 T olive oil
1 large portobello mushroom cap, thinly sliced
½ t coriander
1 T sambal oelek (chili paste; see page 29)
2 c full-flavored chicken stock
1 can coconut milk (Be sure to use unsweetened coconut milk—not "cream of coconut.")
1 9-oz package refrigerated mushroom- or crabmeat-filled tortellini
1 T fresh basil, snipped
1 c heavy cream
1 medium tomato, chopped, for garnish (optional)

In a medium saucepan, cook the shallot, jalapeño pepper, curry powder, and garlic in olive oil about 1 minute, until the shallot is tender. Add the portobello and coriander, and cook 2 more minutes. Stir in the sambal oelek and chicken stock. Bring to a boil. Reduce heat and simmer, covered, for about 5 minutes.

Stir in the coconut milk, tortellini, and basil. Cook and stir about 5 minutes more, or until the pasta is tender but still firm. Stir in the cream and cook until the soup is heated through; do not boil.

Garnish with chopped tomato, if desired. Ladle the soup into bowls and enjoy!

Potato Leek Soup with Crabmeat and Chive Blossoms

Although there are many traditional recipes for potato leek soup, my absolute favorite is this one, with the added cream cheese. It's one of the soups I make for myself when I need true comfort food. Adding Maine crabmeat makes it a filling main dish, but it's also wonderful without.
Serves 6

1 leek
1 sweet onion
10 scallions
8 T butter
4 T vegetable bouillon paste
7 small (about 2 lb) Maine potatoes, chopped
5 c water
8 oz cream cheese
1 c light cream
1 12-oz can evaporated milk
2 c milk
2 c Maine crabmeat
1½ c freshly grated Parmesan cheese (optional)
salt and pepper, to taste
fresh chive blossoms (optional, if available)

Slice the leek vertically. Completely remove the roots and the dark green leaves. Separate the inner layers and rinse thoroughly.

Finely mince the leek, onion, and scallions. Melt butter in a medium saucepan over medium heat. Add the leek, onion, scallions, and vegetable bouillon. Cook until the vegetables are soft. Add the potatoes and water, and cook until potatoes are fork-tender.

Using a potato masher, thoroughly break up the potatoes until very few lumps remain. Add the cream cheese and stir until it melts.

Warm the cream and evaporated and whole milk in a saucepan over medium heat. Add the warmed cream and milk to the soup, and stir until they are incorporated. Add the crabmeat and optional Parmesan cheese, if desired. Add salt and pepper to taste.

Rinse the chive blossoms and pat dry. Break them apart into tiny pieces. Ladle the soup into bowls and garnish each with a sprinkle of chive blossoms. Delicious!

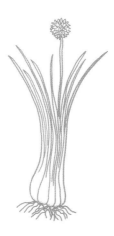

Pub-Style Cheddar and Ale Soup with Beer Bread

Pemaquid Ale is a Scottish-style hearty brew produced in midcoast Maine by the Sheepscot Valley Brewing Company. If you save the bottle, owner and brewer Steve Gorrill will refill it for you for a small fee. Pemaquid Ale and Katahdin Cheddar from the State of Maine Cheese Company are a match made in heaven. (See appendix for addresses.)
Serves 8

3 slices bacon, diced
2 c chopped Vidalia onion
4 T flour
1 t dry mustard
1 T chicken bouillon paste or powder
2 c chicken stock
2 c hearty dark ale
4 c diced Maine potatoes
4 c grated well-aged cheddar cheese
½ c whipping cream
½ t salt
½ t freshly ground white pepper

Beer Bread:
Makes one round loaf (serves 8)
  2 T dry yeast
  2 c hearty ale—preferably Pemaquid Ale
  2 c finely shredded sharp cheddar cheese
  3 eggs
  1 t salt
  1½ t baking soda
  2 T butter, melted
  2 T minced garlic
  5 c flour
  2 T butter, melted

In a large saucepan, sauté bacon over medium heat until crispy. Remove the bacon with a slotted spoon and drain on a paper-towel–lined plate.

Add the onion to the saucepan and cook over medium heat for 5 minutes, or until tender. Add the flour and dry mustard and cook for 2 minutes, stirring constantly. Add the bouillon, stock, and ale. Increase the heat and bring the soup to a boil. Whisk until the soup is thick. Add potatoes and cook until they are fork-tender.

Reduce the heat and add the cheese. Stir until the cheese melts. Stir in the cream, salt, and pepper—do not let the soup boil. Serve with Beer Bread.

Mix the yeast and ale and set aside. In a large bowl, combine cheese, eggs, salt, baking soda, 2 tablespoons of melted butter, and garlic. Mix well.

Add half of the flour and all of the yeast/ale mixture. When combined, add the rest of the flour and knead 5 to 10 minutes. Cover the bowl and let the dough rise.

When the dough has doubled in size, form it into a round loaf and place it on a greased sheet pan. Let the dough rise again until doubled in bulk.

Preheat oven to 350 degrees F. Bake bread for 30 to 40 minutes, until it is light brown.

Brush with the remaining melted butter. Let the bread cool before slicing

Broccoli and Cheddar Soup

The State of Maine Cheese Company (see appendix) has a wonderful assortment of cheeses that they've flavored with herbs and spices. I love using their Katahdin Cheddar. It melts beautifully and adds a sumptuous flavor. This soup is especially nice served in a small, hollowed-out crusty boule.
Serves 6 generously

1 T butter
1 c finely chopped onion
2 c chicken stock
5 lb fresh broccoli, finely chopped
8 oz cream cheese
1 c heavy cream
1 T chicken bouillon paste or powder
1 t salt
black pepper, 10 or so turns of a pepper mill
dash of nutmeg
2¼ c shredded sharp cheddar cheese

Melt butter in a large saucepan over medium heat. Add the onion and sauté until it's translucent.

Add the chicken stock and broccoli. Heat to a simmer and cook 15 minutes.

Add the cream cheese and cream and stir over low heat until the cream cheese melts. Stir in the bouillon, salt, pepper, and nutmeg. Add 2 cups of the cheddar cheese and heat on low, stirring constantly until it melts and blends into the soup.

Using an immersion blender, purée the soup in the pan to the consistency you desire. You may also purée the soup in small batches in a blender. Return the soup to the pan, stir well, and keep warm on very low heat.

When you are ready to serve, garnish the soup with the remaining cheddar cheese and cooked broccoli florets, if desired.

Pesto Soup with Spicy Sausage and Pignoli

This robust soup is spicy and filled with the warm, rich flavors of garlic and basil.

Serves 6 to 8

6 links spicy sausage
1 large onion, chopped
6 cloves garlic, finely minced
4 c beef broth
2 large Maine potatoes, peeled and cubed
1 T chopped fresh basil or 1 t dried
½ c pesto
2 15-oz cans cannellini beans, drained
8 c baby spinach
½ c heavy cream (optional)
½ t salt
2 t sugar
1 t freshly ground pepper

Garnish:
6 T pignoli (pine nuts)
8 oz Parmesan cheese, grated

Remove the casing from the sausage and discard. In a large saucepan, brown the sausage, breaking it up into bite-sized pieces. Add the onion and garlic. Cook over medium heat until the onion is translucent. Add the broth, potato, and basil. Stir to combine. Bring to a boil, reduce heat, and simmer until potato is fork-tender, about 20 minutes. Add the pesto, cannellini beans, and spinach. Cover and cook until the spinach wilts. Add cream (if you wish), salt, sugar, and pepper. Stir to distribute the ingredients evenly.

Serve sprinkled with pignoli and Parmesan.

STEWS

Stews are the backbone of family cooking. Chunky and hearty, they are easy to make. These warm, filling staples can include leftovers you've got in the fridge; substitute freely. Use your imagination and create a stew for your family that you all will enjoy.

Smoked Seafood Stew—A Special Occasion Bouillabaisse

Bouillabaisse is a traditional French seafood stew made from tomatoes, onion, wine, garlic, saffron, herbs, fish, and shellfish. Using smoked seafood along with fresh fish gives an unusual depth of flavor. Ducktrap River Fish Farm (see appendix) makes a wonderful array of smoked seafood.

Serves 8

4 c cooked jasmine rice prepared with 1 T chicken bouillon in the cooking water

1 t saffron threads

½ c dry sherry or white wine

4 T olive oil

1 large Vidalia onion, diced

3 shallots, minced

2 carrots, diced

6 garlic cloves, minced

4 c canned diced tomatoes, with liquid

3 c fish stock, clam juice, or chicken stock

4 T tomato paste

2 t salt

1 t thyme

1 t basil

¼ c fresh parsley

strips of zest from one orange, cut with a paring knife, not a zester

black pepper, 10 twists of a pepper grinder

1 lb haddock or cod, cut in 2-inch pieces

1 c smoked or fresh shrimp

1 c smoked or fresh scallops

4 oz (about 12) smoked clams

4 oz (about 12) smoked mussels

1 to 2 c (2 small) squid (calamari), cleaned and sliced into rings; thawed, if previously frozen

Garnish:

garlic-infused olive oil

parsley sprigs

red pepper flakes

Prepare the jasmine rice according to package directions, adding the chicken bouillon to the cooking water. Keep the cooked rice warm while you prepare the stew.

Add saffron to the wine and set aside. Heat the oil in a large stockpot over low heat. Sauté onion, shallots, carrot, and garlic in the oil until lightly golden. Add tomatoes with liquid, stock or clam juice, tomato paste, and seasonings, including the saffron-infused wine. Bring to a boil. Lower the heat and simmer for 15 minutes.

Add the fish, shrimp, scallops, clams, and mussels. Simmer 10 minutes. Add the squid last, mix, and simmer 10 minutes.

Serve hot in large bowls over ½ cup jasmine rice. Top each serving with a drizzle of garlic oil, a sprig of parsley, and a pinch (or more) of the red pepper flakes.

Whole-Grain Vegetable Stew

Here is a way to get your fiber and vitamins in one tasty cup. This recipe allows you to use the vegetables you like and the grains you have on hand. I've recommended a few, but look at the total amount and improvise with what you've got available. I like to mix it up to have a different texture each time.
Serves 6

1 T butter
1 large onion, chopped
1 T minced fresh garlic
6 c vegetable stock
2 T vegetable bouillon paste or powder
1 c assorted grains (see sidebar for one of many possible combinations)
2 baby carrots, chopped
2 c peeled and diced rutabagas
1 c peeled and diced turnip
2 c thinly sliced and chopped red cabbage
¼ c finely chopped fresh basil or 2 t dried basil
1 T fresh thyme or 1 t dried thyme
¼ c chopped fresh parsley
1 t salt
½ t freshly ground black pepper

In a large saucepan, melt the butter over medium heat and cook the onion until tender, about 5 minutes.

Add the garlic, stock, bouillon, grains, and the remaining vegetables, except cabbage; bring to a boil. Reduce the heat, cover, and simmer for 30 minutes.

Add the cabbage and herbs. Simmer 15 minutes, or until the vegetables and grains are all tender.

Add the parsley, adjust the seasonings, and serve.

These grains make a delicious combination:

¼ c quinoa, rinsed	rice
3 T pearl barley	3 T red lentils
3 T long-grain brown	3 T black rice

Lamb Stew with Rosemary and Garlic

I t is always a treat to purchase lamb from a local farm, raised without antibiotics or growth hormones—just grain, grass, and sunshine. Superb! Winterport Winery's Apple Wine is excellent in this recipe (see appendix).
Serves 10

2 lb lamb stew meat, diced
4 bay leaves
1 t Maine sea salt
¼ c olive oil
3 c chopped potatoes
2 c diced onion
2 c sliced carrots
2 c diced celery
2 c diced parsnips
6 c chicken stock
2 c white wine
6 cloves garlic
3 rosemary stems
1 t oregano
4 T butter, softened
2 T olive oil
4 T flour
¼ c chopped fresh mint leaves
salt and freshly ground black pepper, to taste

Place lamb in a large pot and cover with cold water. Add bay leaves and salt. Bring to a boil and simmer 2 hours. Skim foam off the top and discard.

In a separate large saucepan, heat ¼ cup of olive oil. Add the potatoes, onion, carrots, celery, and parsnips. Sauté 15 minutes Add the cooked lamb and its broth, chicken stock, wine, garlic, rosemary, and oregano. Bring to a boil and simmer one hour.

In a small sauté pan, melt the butter with 2 table-spoons of olive oil. Stir in the flour and let it cook until lightly golden. Stir this roux into the stew until it is thickened and bubbly.

Turn off the heat and remove the large rosemary stems. Add mint and season with salt and pepper to taste. Serve immediately.

All Day No-Fuss Beef Stew

A slow cooker is a simple and helpful kitchen appliance. Fill the cooker and set the temperature in the morning, then come home at the end of the day to delicious aromas— with dinner practically on the table.
Serves 4

3 T flour
1 t Old Bay Seasoning
2 lb pot roast
1 T olive oil
1 large onion, sliced
½ c water
2 c baby carrots
1 c chopped celery
4 T beef bouillon paste or powder
2 T chicken bouillon paste
1 clove garlic, minced
1 large Maine potato, chopped
1 large sweet potato, chopped
4 T flour
4 T butter, softened

Place 3 tablespoons of flour and the Old Bay Seasoning in a large plastic ziplock bag. Seal and shake to combine. Rinse the pot roast and pat dry with paper towels. Place pot roast in the bag with the flour. Seal and shake to coat the meat.

In a medium skillet, heat the olive oil over medium heat. Remove the roast from the bag and gently place it in the skillet. Brown the meat on all sides.

Remove the meat from the pan and place it in a slow cooker. Place the onion in the skillet and cook for 2 minutes. Add the water to the skillet and scrape all of the brown bits of flavor off of the bottom. Pour the onion and water over the meat in the slow cooker. Add the carrots, celery, bouillon pastes or powder, garlic, potato, and sweet potato to the slow cooker. Add enough water to completely cover the ingredients. Cover with the slow cooker lid and cook on low for 6 hours. Skim any foam from the top of the stew and discard.

Just before you're ready to serve, you'll need to cut the meat and thicken the stew. Remove the pot roast and place it on a deep platter. In a small bowl, mix 4 tablespoons of flour and the butter to make a smooth paste. Add to the stew. Stir until no lumps of flour remain and the stew is thick.

Trim any fat off of the meat. Cut the roast into bite-sized pieces and carefully return the meat to the slow cooker. Stir to combine, adjust seasonings to your taste, and serve.

Kitchen Sink Stew

The fine men and women who brave frigid water and endure the backbreaking physical labor it takes to put our favorite seafood on our tables need meals that will help them keep their energy up. Here's one dish that does the trick. You can substitute an equal quantity of mirepoix (page 13) for the onion, bell pepper, carrot, and celery. Filé powder is made from sassafras leaves and is used to thicken the stew. Winterport Winery Dry Pear wine is an excellent choice for this recipe (see appendix).
Serves 8 to 10

1 lb chicken thighs, skinless and boneless, cut into bite-size chunks
2 lemons, halved
2 T olive oil
1 c chopped onion
1 red or green bell pepper, chopped
1 c chopped carrot
1 c chopped celery
1 lb turkey kielbasa, cut into bite-sized pieces
2 T minced garlic
1 c Maine clams (about 10), shucked
1 c white wine
8 c chicken broth
1 lb Maine crabmeat
1 lb Maine shrimp, peeled
1 c corn
2 c chopped fresh kale
1 15-oz can small butter beans, drained
1 28-oz can diced tomatoes
1 t dried thyme leaves
1 t freshly ground black pepper
½ t salt
2 T chicken bouillon paste or powder
2 t Old Bay Seasoning
2 bay leaves
1 c long grain rice
2 t filé powder

2 T butter
1 T olive oil
3 T flour
10 scallions, thinly sliced, for garnish

In a large saucepan, heat 2 cups of water. Add the chicken and lemon halves. Poach the chicken until it is cooked through. Remove chicken with a slotted spoon and set it aside.

In another large saucepan, heat the oil over medium heat. Add the onion, bell pepper, carrots, and celery. Sauté 5 minutes or until the onion is translucent. Add the kielbasa and cook another 5 minutes. Add the garlic, clams, and wine. Reduce heat to low and cook covered for 15 minutes.

Add the chicken broth, crabmeat, shrimp, corn, kale, beans, tomatoes, thyme, black pepper, salt, bouillon, Old Bay Seasoning, bay leaves, and rice. Stir well to combine. Cover and simmer 30 minutes, or until the rice is tender.

Add the reserved chicken and the filé powder. In a small sauté pan, melt the butter with the olive oil. Stir in the flour and let it cook until lightly golden. Add this roux to the stew and stir until the stew is thickened and bubbly.

Serve topped with scallions.

Winter Solstice Stew

A friend reminded me recently that we are all made mostly of water, and water is as old as time. So we, in turn, are as old as time. The wisdom we achieve is more than the sum of our experiences. It's how we choose to nourish both our minds and our bodies. This stew gives us a way to enjoy many of the Earth's nourishing root vegetables.
Serves 6 to 8

2 lb sweet potatoes
2 lb Maine potatoes
1 parsnip
1 rutabaga
2 sweet onions
3 carrots
1 lb butternut squash
5 c chicken or vegetable stock
¼ c Maine maple syrup
⅛ t cinnamon
⅛ t nutmeg
⅛ t ground ginger

Peel and chop the first seven ingredients. Put them in a soup pot, along with the stock. Bring to a boil, reduce the heat, and simmer for 60 minutes, or until the vegetables are soft.

Now is the time to blend your soup—leaving some chunks for texture. An immersion blender is perfect for blending the soup right in the pan. If you use a regular blender instead, process the soup briefly by the cupful, being careful not to burn yourself, and return the processed soup to the pan.

Stir in the maple syrup and spices before serving.

Chicken Stew with Parsleyed Squash Dumplings

Traditional chicken stew: good for the body, good for the soul. This recipe is an old favorite. It's thick and full of chunky goodness. Buttery, light, and easy to make, dumplings are a quick addition to any bubbling soup. The squash gives these dumplings a golden glow.

Serves 4 to 6

1 5-lb chicken, cut into quarters
2 lb chicken thighs, bone-in
1 large onion, peeled and quartered
10 peppercorns
4 sprigs parsley
4 cloves garlic, coarsely chopped
1 Granny Smith apple, halved
1 carrot, coarsely chopped
2 celery ribs, coarsely chopped
6 c water, more or less
2 lb potatoes
1 lb carrots, peeled
6 celery ribs
3 T chicken bouillon
¼ c butter
¼ c flour
½ t salt
½ t freshly ground black pepper
1 c corn
1 c peas
¼ c finely chopped fresh parsley

In a large saucepan, place the chicken, onion, peppercorns, sprigs of parsley, garlic, apple, chopped carrot, and 2 ribs of chopped celery. Add enough water to cover the ingredients by at least two inches; the amount will depend on the size of the pot you are using. Bring to a boil and simmer, covered, for 45 minutes.

While the chicken mixture cooks, cut the potatoes, carrots, and 6 celery ribs into bite-sized pieces.

Skim off and discard any foam from the top of the stew. Pour the entire contents of the pot through a colander into another large pot. Set the solids aside to cool. Place this second pot on the stove and bring the contents to a rolling boil. Cook 10 minutes.

When the chicken in the colander is cool enough to handle, remove all of the meat from the bones. Tear or cut the meat into bite-sized pieces and set aside. Discard the bones, skin, and any remaining solids.

Stir the bouillon into the boiling stock. Add the cut-up potatoes, carrots, and celery. Reduce heat to medium and cook the vegetables until they are fork-tender.

Melt the butter in a small sauté pan. Stir in the flour and cook until the mixture, or roux, is lightly golden. Add the roux to the stew and stir until the stew is thickened and bubbly. Taste the broth and add additional bouillon, salt, or pepper, as needed.

Add the reserved chicken to the pan. Add the corn, peas, and parsley. Cook another 10 minutes.

Prepare the dough for the Parsleyed Squash Dumplings (next page), cook them in the stew, and serve.

Parsleyed Squash Dumplings:
- 3 c flour
- 1 teaspoon salt
- 2 T baking powder
- 5 T butter
- 1 c light cream
- ½ c puréed squash
- ¼ c finely chopped fresh parsley

Combine the flour, salt, and baking powder in a medium bowl.

In a small saucepan, bring the butter, cream, and squash just to a simmer. Add the cream mixture and parsley to the dry ingredients. Stir with a fork until the mixture just comes together.

Divide the dough into about 18 small pieces. Roll each piece into a small, roughly shaped ball. Carefully place the dumplings on the surface of the bubbling stew. Cover and simmer 12 minutes. Serve immediately.

Fisherman's Stew

This tomatoey seafood stew is cooked slowly to meld the flavors. Winterport Winery Demi-Pear is an excellent choice for the white wine (see appendix).
Serves 8

- 3½ c or 1 28-oz can crushed tomatoes, with juice
- 1 c tomato sauce
- 1 c chopped onion
- 1 c dry white wine
- 3 T olive oil
- 4 cloves garlic, minced
- ½ c chopped fresh parsley
- 1 red bell pepper, chopped
- 1 Anaheim pepper, finely chopped
- ½ t Maine sea salt
- ½ t freshly ground black pepper
- 1 t thyme
- 1 T basil
- 2 t oregano
- 1 t paprika
- ¼ t cayenne pepper
- 1 c water
- 8 oz Maine shrimp
- 8 oz haddock or salmon filet, boneless and skinless
- 8 oz scallops
- 8 oz mussels
- 8 oz clams
- ¾ c heavy cream

Place tomatoes, tomato sauce, onion, wine, oil, garlic, parsley, red pepper, Anaheim pepper, sea salt, black pepper, thyme, basil, oregano, paprika, cayenne, and water in a slow cooker. Cover and cook 6 to 8 hours on low heat.

Thirty minutes before serving, add the shrimp, fish, scallops, mussels, and clams. Set the heat on high. Stir occasionally during the last 20 minutes. Heat just until the seafood is cooked through.

Add the cream and stir. Serve with a crusty bread.

Chicken Nacho Grande Stew

Here is a stew version of ever-popular nachos, with spicy, creamy, and hearty flavors in every bite. Served atop a bed of blue corn tortilla chips, it's crunchy, too. Shipwreck Galley's Cherry & Brandy Salsa works beautifully in this recipe (see appendix).

Serves 6 to 8

2 T olive oil
1 large onion, diced
1 t dried chipotle chili pepper
1 T chili powder
2 t cumin
3 T minced garlic
2 Anaheim chili peppers, finely chopped
1 jalapeño pepper, finely chopped
4 c cooked chicken
2 c cooked black beans
5 c chicken or beef stock

4 large tomatoes, diced
2 c tomato purée
2 c canned diced tomato, with juice
1 c fruit salsa
3 T chopped cilantro
1 t oregano
2 t white pepper
1 t salt
juice of 1 lime
blue corn chips

In a large saucepan, heat the oil over medium heat and sauté the onion, chili powders, cumin, and garlic. Sauté until the onion is translucent. Add the Anaheim and jalapeño peppers. Cook, stirring often, for 5 minutes.

Add the cooked chicken, black beans, stock, all the tomatoes, salsa, cilantro, oregano, pepper, and salt. Stir to combine well and cook over low heat for 40 minutes.

Just before serving, add the lime juice and adjust seasonings to taste.

To serve, place blue corn chips in each bowl and top with stew. If desired, spoon salsa on top, drizzle with Cumin Crema, top with avocado, and sprinkle with scallions and cheese.

Cumin Crema
    8 oz sour cream
    1 t cumin
    ¼ t cayenne
    juice of 1 lime

In a small bowl, combine the sour cream, cumin, cayenne, and lime juice. Mix well.

Toppings (optional):
    1 c fruit salsa
    2 avocados, coarsely chopped
    6 scallions, thinly sliced
    1 lb pepper Jack or queso blanco cheese, grated

Venison Stew

When the weather turns cold, nothing warms your bones better than a hot bowl of thick, meaty stew. This recipe can also be made with beef.
Serves 10 to 12

2 lb venison, cut into 1-inch chunks
1 c chopped onion
4 medium Maine potatoes, chopped
½ lb tiny button mushrooms
1 c chopped baby carrots
4 c hearty beef stock
2 T beef bouillon
½ t garlic powder
⅛ t oregano
½ c flour, mixed with ½ c cold water
salt and pepper

In a medium heavy-bottomed saucepan, sauté the venison and onion just enough to sear the outside of the meat. Place the meat, potatoes, onion, mushrooms, carrots, stock, bouillon, garlic, and oregano in a slow cooker. Cook on medium for 4 hours.

Mix the flour and water and add to the stew. Adjust seasonings with salt and pepper.

Cook for 6 more hours on low. It's okay to let it stew longer if you've got time before dinner. Cooking longer will allow the stew to thicken, and the meat will be even more tender.

Chicken Cacciatore Stew with Garlic Toasts

Our friends Bryce and Dianne served a delicious chicken cacciatore for the long-awaited first dinner at their new home. It was almost stewlike and started a discussion about what stew really is. This variation gives you both the complex flavors of cacciatore and the thick, delicious quality of stew.
Serves 8 to 10

¾ c flour
½ t salt
½ t oregano
1 t paprika
10 chicken thighs, boneless and skinless
2 T extra-virgin olive oil
1 medium red bell pepper, diced
1 medium green bell pepper, diced
1 medium orange bell pepper, diced
1 medium yellow bell pepper, diced
1 large onion, diced (about 2 c)
4 cloves garlic, minced
1 c white wine
6 c diced fresh or canned tomatoes, with
    their juice
2 c chicken broth
1 small bottle capers (about ⅓ c), drained
¼ c tomato paste
1 T oregano
½ c finely chopped fresh parsley
1 t salt
1 t freshly ground black pepper

Place flour, salt, oregano, and paprika in a large ziplock bag. Close the bag and shake to combine. Cut the chicken into 1-inch pieces and add to the bag with the flour mixture. Close the bag and shake it again to coat the chicken completely.

Heat the oil in a large saucepan over medium heat. Add the peppers, onion, and garlic to the saucepan. Cook, stirring often, until the onion is translucent. Add the chicken, leaving the excess flour in the ziplock bag. Continue cooking until the chicken is lightly browned and almost done, about 10 minutes.

Add the remaining flour from the ziplock bag. Stir well to incorporate the flour, coating all of the chicken and veggies.

Deglaze the pan with the wine. Use a wooden spatula or spoon to scrape the sides and bottom of the pan to incorporate all the brown crispy bits. Stir well to remove any lumps of flour. Simmer until the liquid is thickened and has reduced by half.

Add the tomatoes, chicken broth, capers, tomato paste, oregano, parsley, salt, and pepper. Simmer, stirring often, for 30 minutes. Make sure you stir all the way down to the bottom of the pan so any stuck bits don't burn.

Garlic Toasts:
    10 slices whole-grain bread
    2 cloves garlic

Toast the slices of bread to a golden brown. Cut the cloves of garlic in half. Rub each slice of toast with the cut side of the garlic, coating the entire slice. This invisible layer of garlic will lend a delicious flavor without adding extra calories or fat.

CHOWDERS AND OTHER THICK SOUPS

Thick and hearty, warm and bubbly. . . These soups will fill you up and keep you going; some of them are elegant enough for a dinner party. Many chowders call for bacon or salt pork. To lessen the fat content, feel free to substitute turkey bacon, or omit the salt pork or bacon altogether, according to your taste.

Maine Clam Chowder

Enjoying a mug of steaming chowder loaded with chunks of seafood, while sitting on a deck with the ocean breeze in your hair—everyone should experience this pleasure. Here is the traditional recipe I first learned. The flavor of the clams comes through, and it's simple, quick to make, and delicious. If you love the taste of smoked seafood, substitute smoked clams—such as those made by Ducktrap River Fish Farm—for the freshly cooked clams.
Serves 4 to 6

10 slices bacon
4 T reserved bacon fat
1 c chopped onion
4 medium potatoes, chopped into bite-sized
   chunks
½ c flour
5 c bottled clam juice
16 oz (2 c) chopped cooked clams
½ c milk
½ c light cream
1 t salt
freshly ground black pepper

In a large saucepan, sauté the bacon until it's crispy. Remove the bacon and place on a paper-towel–lined plate to drain. Reserve 4 tablespoons of the bacon fat in the saucepan and spoon out the rest for use in another recipe. When the bacon is cool enough to handle, crumble it into a bowl and set it aside.

Cook the onion in the saucepan over low heat in the bacon fat until the onion is translucent. Do not brown. Add the potatoes and cook for another 5 to 8 minutes, until they are fork-tender. Remove the potatoes and onion with a slotted spoon; place the mixture in a bowl and set aside.

Stir the flour into the fat in the saucepan and scrape up any brown bits from the bottom with a whisk. Add the clam juice and whisk constantly until the flour is completely incorporated. (You don't want any lumps.) Continue cooking on low heat until thick.

Return the potatoes and onion to the thickened liquid. Add the clams, milk, cream, salt, and pepper, and stir well to incorporate. Warm the mixture, but do not let it boil. Ladle the chowder into bowls and top with the reserved bacon.

New England Corn Chowder

This recipe is nontraditional but quick and yummy. Corn chowder tastes wonderful reheated, and the recipe is easily doubled for a crowd.
Serves 6 to 8

salt pork, a piece 1-inch by 1-inch by 3 inches,
   or 4 slices bacon
1 c chopped onion
1 c chicken or vegetable stock
4 c diced potatoes
2 c light cream
2 c evaporated milk
2 c sweet corn, frozen or canned
2 12-oz cans creamed corn
½ t salt
freshly ground black pepper, to taste

Slice the salt pork or bacon into thin strips and finely dice. Sauté in a medium saucepan until brown and crispy. Remove with a slotted spoon and drain on a paper-towel–lined plate.

Add onion to the bacon fat and cook until translucent. Add the stock and potatoes. Simmer 20 minutes or until the potatoes are fork-tender.

Add the cream, evaporated milk, sweet corn, creamed corn, salt, and pepper. Heat until just simmering; do not boil.

Serve topped with the crunchy salt pork or bacon bits and oyster crackers or biscuits. Store in the refrigerator up to four days.

Fish Chowder with Caramelized Onion Squares

I've been eating this chowder all my life. Little bits of salt pork cracklings garnish the finished chowder. Salt pork historically has been the base flavoring for all chowders. The tasty, crunchy tidbits add saltiness, texture, and fullness of flavor. The Caramelized Onion Squares add just the right crispy texture to complete the meal.
Serves 10

salt pork, a piece 1 inch by 1 inch by 3 inches
2 c chopped onion
3 c fish stock
2 sprigs fresh thyme
5 medium Maine potatoes, cut in bite-sized chunks
4 T butter
4 T flour
1 lb haddock, cod, or cusk fillets
3 c light cream
1 c heavy cream
½ t salt
½ t freshly ground black pepper

Slice the salt pork into thin strips and finely dice it. Sauté the pork in a medium saucepan until it is brown and crispy. Remove with a slotted spoon and drain on a paper-towel–lined plate.

Add the onion to the fat in the pan and cook on low until the onion is translucent. Add the stock, thyme, and potatoes. Simmer 20 minutes or until the potatoes are fork-tender.

Melt the butter in a small sauté pan. Whisk in the flour and cook until it is golden. Gently add this mixture, or roux, to your saucepan once the potatoes are cooked. Stir until the liquid is thick and no lumps of roux remain.

Add the fish; cover and simmer until the fish is tender. Add the creams and heat slowly. Season to taste with salt and pepper. Remove the stems remaining from the sprigs of thyme. Stir and simmer until the chowder is thick and bubbly.

Turn off the heat and let stand, covered, for 45 minutes or put it in the refrigerator until you are ready to eat it.

When it's time to enjoy the chowder, reheat it gently and do not allow it to boil. Remember to adjust the seasonings before serving, and garnish each bowl with a sprinkle of salt pork cracklings.

Caramelized Onion Squares:
Yield: 12 squares
2 T butter
3 medium Vidalia or other sweet onions, cut in half and thinly sliced
1 t chicken bouillon
1 t Maine maple syrup
¼ c water
1 sheet puff pastry, thawed if frozen
sea salt and freshly ground pepper, to taste

Preheat oven to 400 degrees F. In a medium skillet, melt the butter. Sauté the onion on low for 5 minutes. Stir in the bouillon and maple syrup.

Continue cooking until the onion is caramel brown. Add ¼ cup hot water. Stir to deglaze the pan and incorporate all of the tasty brown bits on the bottom of the pan.

Unfold the puff pastry sheet on a sheet pan. Press any seams together. Cover the pastry entirely with a layer of the caramelized onion. Sprinkle with sea salt and pepper. Bake 15 to 20 minutes, or until the puff pastry is flaky, crispy, and browned on the bottom.

Remove the pastry from the pan onto a cutting board. Slice into 12 squares and serve hot.

Lobster Arborio Soup with Cognac and White Truffle Oil

Lobster meat and truffle oil are a sumptuous and elegant combination.
Serves 4 to 6

4 lobster tails, shelled but uncooked
6½ c chicken broth
4 T white truffle oil
1 c chopped sweet carrots
⅓ c chopped shallots
1 c arborio rice
⅓ c cognac
1 c lobster or fish stock
½ c whipping cream
½ c chopped fresh chives
salt and pepper, to taste

Have a bowl of ice water on hand. Heat a large saucepan of water to a boil and add the lobster tails. Reduce the heat and simmer the lobster until it is cooked through, about 8 minutes.

Immediately place the lobster in the bowl of ice water to stop the cooking process. Cut the meat into bite-sized pieces and set it aside.

In a large saucepan, bring 3½ cups of the chicken broth to a simmer. Heat 1 tablespoon of the truffle oil in a large, heavy saucepan over medium heat. Add the carrots and shallots and cook, stirring, for 2 minutes.

Add the rice. Cook and stir for 2 minutes more. Slowly stir in the cognac. Reduce the heat to low and simmer, stirring constantly, for 3 minutes or until the rice absorbs the liquid. Add the lobster or fish stock and ½ cup of the chicken broth. Simmer, continuing to add chicken broth ¼ cup at a time until all the liquid is incorporated. Stir often. This process will take about 25 minutes. Cook until the rice is just tender and creamy.

Add the lobster and cream and gently heat through. Remove from the heat and stir in the remaining 2 tablespoons of truffle oil and the chives. Season with salt and pepper.

Golden Lentil Soup with Mini Lamb Meatballs and Mint Drizzle

Enjoy tender lamb in this easily prepared soup. The orange lentils cook quickly. Look for them in the bulk section of grocery and specialty stores.
Serves 8

Soup:

3 T olive oil
2 c chopped red onion
1 T turmeric
2 t cumin
1 c diced carrot
5 T minced garlic
½ c finely chopped celery
1 lb golden lentils
10 c chicken stock, warmed
1 T chicken bouillon paste
salt and freshly ground pepper, to taste
¼ t cayenne
1 T finely chopped fresh parsley
1 T finely chopped fresh thyme

Meatballs:

¾ c fresh bread crumbs
⅓ c whole milk
2 eggs, lightly beaten
1½ lbs ground Maine lamb
1 c ground blanched almonds
⅓ c chopped onion
⅓ c coarsely chopped golden raisins
3 T minced garlic
3 T chopped fresh parsley
3 T chopped fresh cilantro
1 t oregano
¼ t cayenne
½ t salt
½ t freshly ground black pepper
3 T olive oil

To prepare the soup:

In a large saucepan, heat the olive oil over low heat. Add the onion, turmeric, and cumin. Cook until you release the aroma of the spices, about 2 minutes. Add the carrot, garlic, and celery. Sauté over medium heat until the onion is translucent, about 5 minutes. Stir in the lentils, chicken stock, and bouillon. Season with salt, pepper, and cayenne. Bring to a boil. Reduce the heat and simmer for 30 minutes, or until the lentils are tender. Skim any foam that forms on the top of the soup as it cooks.

Using a potato masher, gently press the lentils to remove most of the lumps. Add parsley and thyme.

To prepare the meatballs:

In a large bowl, soak the bread crumbs in milk until they've absorbed all the liquid.

Add the eggs, lamb, almonds, onion, raisins, garlic, parsley, cilantro, oregano, cayenne, salt, and pepper. Moisten your hands with olive oil and combine all of the ingredients in the bowl until the mixture has a uniform appearance. Form the meat mixture into 60 or so 1-inch meatballs.

Heat 2 tablespoons of olive oil in a large sauté pan over medium heat. Arrange the meatballs in a single layer in the pan. Brown the meatballs, turning often to brown all sides, about 8 to 10 minutes.

To serve, ladle the soup into bowls. Top with 4 or 5 meatballs and spoon Mint Drizzle (next page) over the top.

Mint Drizzle:
Yield: about 1 cup
- 1 c plain yogurt
- 1 lemon, juice and zest
- 1 T chopped fresh mint leaves
- 1 t Maine maple syrup
- ¼ t salt

In a small bowl, combine all ingredients. Chill.

Lobster, Crab, Shrimp, and Vegetable Soup

This soup combines the most delicious products of both garden and sea in one bowl.
Serves 8 to 10

- 6 c water
- 1 c chopped sweet onion
- 2 c chopped celery
- 2 large Maine potatoes, chopped
- 1 T chopped fresh thyme
- 3 bay leaves
- 4 1½-lb Maine lobsters
- 2 c frozen peas
- ¼ c finely chopped celery
- 2 c diced carrots
- 1 onion, finely chopped
- 3 large Maine potatoes, chopped
- 2 c chicken stock
- 2 c vegetable stock
- 2 T chicken or vegetable bouillon paste or powder
- 2 c heavy cream
- 1 t garlic powder
- 1 T fresh thyme
- 2 c Maine crabmeat
- 1 c Maine shrimp
- ½ c marsala wine
- salt and pepper, to taste

In a large stockpot, heat the water. Add the onion, celery, potatoes, thyme, and bay leaves. Bring to a rolling boil. Submerge the lobsters and cook for 15 minutes. Remove the lobsters and set them aside to cool.

When the lobsters are cool enough to handle, remove the meat from the shells. Chop into bite-sized pieces and set aside.

Strain the stock and return it to the stockpot, saving the vegetables. Purée the cooked vegetables and set them aside.

Place the remaining ingredients, except the seafood and puréed vegetables, into the stockpot. Bring to a boil, lower the heat, and simmer for 1 to 1½ hours, stirring occasionally.

Add the puréed vegetables to the stockpot and stir to combine. Gently stir in the lobster, crabmeat, and shrimp. Add salt and pepper to taste. Serve with crusty bread for dunking.

Ducktrap River Smoked Seafood Chowder

This is truly a special dish for the smoked seafood aficionado. Ducktrap River Fish Farm (see appendix) offers a superb assortment. Feel free to mix and match seafoods to suit your taste.
Serves 8

1 6-oz piece smoked trout, skin removed
4 oz smoked salmon, skin removed
3 T unsalted butter
1 c chopped red onion
3 c fish stock
6 medium Maine russet potatoes, cut in bite-sized chunks
1 c corn
4 oz smoked shrimp
4 oz smoked scallops
4 oz smoked mussels
4 oz smoked clams
½ t paprika
3 c light cream
2 c heavy cream

salt and freshly ground black pepper, to taste
2 scallions, thinly sliced, for garnish (optional)

Break up the trout and salmon into bite-sized pieces. Place butter and onion in a large heavy-bottomed saucepan and cook on low until the onion is soft.

Add the stock and potatoes and simmer 20 minutes, or until the potatoes are fork-tender.

Add the corn, all of the seafood, paprika, and the light and heavy cream. Heat on low for 15 minutes. Season with salt and pepper.

When you dish up the chowder, make sure each guest receives a little of each type of seafood. Serve garnished with the scallion, if desired.

Baked Potato Look-Alike Soup

Baked potatoes were a popular dinner item in our house when I was growing up. Mom would bake a big potato for each of us and place bowls of cheese, vegetables, crumbled bacon, and sour cream on the table for us to use to "decorate" our potatoes. This soup takes all that flavor and puts it into one pot with a twist: The taste of the potato is there without all the carbs.
Serves 4 to 6

1 medium head cauliflower
3 T olive oil
½ t salt
freshly ground pepper, 10 twists of a pepper mill
2 slices bacon, coarsely chopped
½ c finely chopped onion
4 c chicken or vegetable stock
3 oz shredded cheddar or Jack cheese
1 c light cream
3 T fresh chopped chives
2 T butter
additional chopped chives and a few T sour
   cream, for garnish

Chop the cauliflower into 1-inch pieces and steam until tender. Using a slotted spoon, place the cauliflower in a 2-quart baking dish. Drizzle with olive oil. Sprinkle with salt and pepper and broil until the cauliflower is golden brown.

In a large saucepan, cook the bacon until crisp. Remove with a slotted spoon to a paper-towel–lined plate to drain.

Add the onion to the bacon fat in the saucepan and cook until translucent. Add the cauliflower and broth. Simmer for 20 minutes, or until the cauliflower is tender.

Using an immersion blender, purée the soup right in the pan, or pour the soup into a food processor or blender, process until smooth, and return it to the pan.

Add the cheese, bacon, cream, and chives, and stir until the cheese melts. Add the butter and stir until it melts.

Serve sprinkled with additional chives and a dollop of sour cream, if you like.

Split Pea Soup with Ham

I've tinkered with this recipe over the last decade. Its simplicity allows each flavor to shine through.
Serves 8 to 10

2 16-oz bags split peas
2 c chopped carrots
1 c chopped onion
2 c chopped potatoes
1 meaty ham bone
2 bay leaves
salt and pepper, to taste
2 c chopped ham, in ½-inch cubes

Place all ingredients except the ham into a large saucepan. Add water up to 2 inches above the ingredients. Bring to a boil over medium heat. Reduce heat and simmer 3 hours, or until peas have cooked down and the soup is slightly thickened.

Remove the ham bone and bay leaves. Use a potato masher to break up any large lumps. Stir in the cubed ham. Serve with slices of crusty bread.

Curried Sweet Potato Soup

At a soup party, a friend gave this soup a try even though she had never liked sweet potatoes. It was her favorite soup of the night. Curry and spiced rum make the flavor complex and scrumptious.
Serves 4 to 6

1 T olive oil
3 scant T curry powder
1 c chopped onion
3 T minced garlic
1 T grated gingerroot
4 c peeled and cubed sweet potatoes
4 c peeled and cubed Maine potatoes
1 t salt
½ t freshly ground white pepper
½ t crushed red pepper
4 c hearty vegetable stock
8 oz cream cheese
3 T spiced rum
sour cream and paprika, for garnish

In a large saucepan, warm the oil over medium-low heat. Add the curry and onion and cook for 5 minutes, stirring often. Add garlic and ginger. Cook for another 3 minutes. Add the potatoes, salt, white and red peppers, and the stock and simmer for 20 minutes, or until the potatoes are fork-tender.

Puree the soup using an immersion blender or food processor. Add the cream cheese and stir over low heat until the cream cheese melts into the soup. Add more stock or water if necessary.

Add the rum and serve immediately, topping each bowl with a dollop of sour cream and a sprinkle of paprika.

Pumpkin, White Bean, and Sausage Soup

Thick, spicy, and savory, this soup sticks to your ribs. The beautiful pumpkin orange color is specked with white beans and meaty sausage. It's great with a slice of thick, crusty bread.
Serves 6

1 lb spicy sausage
½ c minced onion
1 T minced garlic
1 c finely chopped mushrooms
1 T oregano
2 c pumpkin purée or 1 15-oz can pumpkin
4 c chicken broth
2 c cooked white beans (navy, cannellini, or butter beans)
1 c edammame (green soy beans)
1 c half-and-half or soy milk
fresh parsley, chopped (optional)

Remove and discard the casing from the sausage. Brown the sausage in a large saucepan, breaking it up into bite-sized pieces. Remove sausage with a slotted spoon and place on a paper-towel–lined plate to drain.

Add the onion, garlic, mushrooms, and oregano to the saucepan. When the onion is translucent, stir in the pumpkin and broth. Return the sausage to the pot, along with the white beans and the edammame. Simmer 30 minutes.

Stir in the half-and-half or soy milk and simmer on low another 15 minutes, stirring often. Taste and adjust seasonings.

Serve sprinkled with parsley, if desired.

Chicken Peanut Saté Soup with Lo Mein Noodles

Peanut soup? Yup! The peanut flavor blends wonderfully with the Far East seasonings in the marinade that gives the chicken its unique flavor. For a variation of this dish, alternate the chicken and chunks of fresh pineapple on skewers and grill until the meat is cooked. Serve them with the soup for dipping.
Serves 6

Marinade:
3 T finely chopped onion
3 T soy sauce
1 t sambal oelek (chili paste; see page 29)
2 t ground ginger
2 T grated gingerroot
1 t lemongrass powder
2 T minced garlic
1 t turmeric
2 t coriander
2 t cumin
1 T sesame oil

Soup:
2 lb chicken thighs, boneless and skinless,
    cut into bite-sized pieces
2 T sesame oil
½ c minced onion
2 T minced garlic
1 c chopped celery
4 T soy sauce
1 t sambal oelek
3 T grated gingerroot
1 T lemongrass powder
1 t turmeric
2 t coriander
2 t cumin
4 c canned chicken broth
2 c chunky peanut butter
1 c smooth peanut butter
16 oz fresh lo mein noodles

Garnish:
chopped peanuts
6 scallions, thinly sliced

Marinate the chicken: Place all of the marinade ingredients in a large ziplock bag. Place the chicken in the bag and massage the marinade into the meat. Carefully press the air out of the bag and zip it closed. Place the bag in a bowl and chill 1 hour.

To make the soup, place the sesame oil in a large, heavy-bottomed saucepan over medium heat. Sauté the chicken until it is cooked through. Remove the chicken from the pan and set aside.

Cook the onion, garlic, and celery until soft, but not brown. Add soy sauce, 1 teaspoon of sambal oelek, ginger, lemongrass, turmeric, coriander, and cumin. Add the chicken broth, stirring constantly, and bring to a boil.

Remove from the heat and add the peanut butter. Stir to blend thoroughly.

Reheat the soup over low heat; do not boil. Add the cooked chicken and heat through.

In a separate pot, cook the lo mein noodles according to package directions. Place a serving of noodles in each bowl and top with soup. Garnish with the chopped peanuts and scallions.

Spring Pea Soup with Shrimp

Spring Pea Soup is made from fresh peas, not dried split peas. It reminds me of the time we were visiting Aunt Nancy and Uncle Lloyd in Aroostook County, when my cousin dumped a truckload of pea vines on their lawn. We all pulled up chairs and shelled peas until the last pod was empty. There were new peas and potatoes for supper.
Serves 4 to 6

¼ c diced bacon
1 T oil
3 T flour
1 c thinly sliced leeks
3 c coarsely chopped Maine potatoes
4 c chicken or vegetable stock
4 c fresh peas
¾ c heavy cream
1 t salt
½ t pepper
1 T snipped chives
1 c (about ½ lb) cooked Maine shrimp

In a large saucepan, cook the bacon until it's crispy. Remove it with a slotted spoon and drain it on a paper-towel–lined plate. Crumble and reserve the bacon for an optional garnish or other use.

Add the oil and flour to the pan and cook for 4 minutes, stirring constantly. Add leeks and cook 4 more minutes. Add the potatoes and stock and bring to a boil. Reduce the heat and simmer for 30 minutes.

Add the peas and cook 5 minutes. Using an immersion blender, purée the soup in the pot; or, process the soup in small batches in a blender, returning the puréed soup to the pot. Stir in the cream, salt, and pepper and stir well. Ladle the soup into bowls and serve garnished with chives and shrimp. If you wish, sprinkle with the reserved bits of crumbled bacon.

Carrot Ginger Soup

The secret to this soup is to use the freshest vegetables you can find: sweet carrots; firm shallots; fragrant ginger.
Serves 4 to 6

3 T unsalted butter
1 c sliced shallots (about 4 large)
1 bay leaf
1 T freshly grated ginger
1 t curry powder
2 t chopped fresh thyme
½ c chopped Maine potato
1½ lb carrots, peeled and finely diced
2 c vegetable broth
½ c apple cider
1 c water
1 T vegetable bouillon paste or powder
1 t salt
½ t freshly ground black pepper

In a large saucepan, melt the butter over low heat and add the shallots, bay leaf, ginger, curry powder, and thyme. Cook, stirring occasionally, until the shallots are soft and pale gold, 8 minutes or so. Add potato, carrots, broth, cider, water, bouillon, salt, and pepper. Bring to a boil and simmer, covered, for about 30 minutes or until the carrots are tender.

When the soup is done, purée it using an immersion blender or food processor.

This is delicious as is, but for a special optional garnish, sprinkle it with Curried Almonds.

Curried Almonds:
Makes about 1 cup
2 T butter, melted
1 t curry powder
dash cayenne pepper
1 t brown sugar
1 c sliced almonds, toasted

In a small sauté pan, melt the butter. Add the curry powder, cayenne pepper, and brown sugar. Cook, stirring constantly until the aroma of the spices is released. Add the almonds and stir to coat. Pour the mixture onto a greased sheet pan to cool. When cool, break up the nuts.

Tipsy Tomato Soup

This soup is reminiscent of the popular vodka sauce served on pasta.
Serves 4 to 6

2 T olive oil
1 c finely minced onion
2 T minced garlic
6 large tomatoes, chopped
2 c canned diced tomatoes, with their juice
2 c tomato sauce
1 c hearty chicken broth
1 c heavy cream
2 t sugar or Splenda sweetener
1 t paprika
½ t red pepper flakes
salt and pepper, to taste

½ c vodka
10 large basil leaves, finely chopped
3 T fresh chopped parsley

In a large saucepan, heat the oil on high and sauté the onion for 5 minutes. Lower the heat, add the garlic, tomatoes, and tomato sauce. Cook 15 minutes more.

Add broth, cream, sugar or Splenda, paprika, red pepper, salt, and pepper. Cook 10 minutes on low heat. Stir in the vodka and basil.

Serve the soup sprinkled with parsley.

Emerald Soup with Crème Fraîche Swirl

Bright green and garlicky, this elegant soup is fit for a king.
Serves 6

8 c leaf spinach, firmly packed
2 T olive oil
2 c chopped white onion
2 T minced garlic
1 c chopped celery
1 t cumin
4 c chicken broth
1 t oregano
2 c diced tomatoes
salt and pepper
crème fraîche, for garnish

Rinse spinach well and remove large stems. In a large saucepan, heat the olive oil over medium heat and sauté the onion, garlic, celery, and cumin for 5 minutes. Reduce heat, add the spinach. Cover and cook 5 minutes more. Add chicken broth and oregano and simmer gently for 15 minutes.

Purée the soup using an immersion blender or food processor. Add the tomatoes, stir, and heat through. Adjust the balance of salt and pepper.

When serving, stir a dollop of crème fraîche into each bowl, to melt into the emerald green soup.

Thick and Hearty Simple Chili

Shipwreck Galley has a fantastic line of spirited salsas made in Maine (see appendix). Their Cherry & Brandy Salsa is delicious on its own, and it also adds a wonderful layer of flavor to this chili.
Serves 4, with leftovers for tomorrow's lunch

1 lb lean ground beef, chicken, or turkey
2 c chopped onion
3 T minced garlic
1 T beef bouillon paste or powder
1 T oregano
1 t cumin
1 t chili powder
1 t cayenne
1 t salt
1 T sugar
1 t freshly ground black pepper
1 c cooked kidney beans, drained
1 c cooked black beans, drained
1 4-oz can tomato paste
1 c puréed tomatoes, canned or fresh

1 c Shipwreck Galley Cherry & Brandy Salsa
  or your favorite fruit salsa
2 c refried beans
1 c corn
1 c cooked chick peas

Garnish:
  shredded cheese
  1 c Shipwreck Galley Cherry & Brandy Salsa
  sour cream
  avocado slices

In a large, heavy-bottomed pan, brown the ground meat over medium heat. Remove excess fat, if necessary. Add the onion and garlic to the pan and cook until the onion is translucent. Add the bouillon, oregano, cumin, chili powder, cayenne, salt, sugar, and black pepper, and mix well. Add the kidney beans, black beans, tomato paste, tomatoes, salsa, and refried beans. Heat and stir well until the refried beans are completely incorporated into the chili. Add the corn and chick peas.

Turn the heat to low and cover, stirring often, until the chili has a creamy, thick consistency. Let the chili simmer 30 minutes or up to 2 hours for the flavors to meld. Be sure to scrape the bottom as you stir so there will not be any burned bits in the chili.

Serve in bowls with shredded cheese, additional salsa, sour cream, and avocado slices on top.

Pasta Fagiola

This Pasta Fagiola is better known as Sacco Fazool. Tony Sacco's famous Pasta Fagiola has been evolving in his family for decades. He shared the recipe with me but left parts of it a secret. I've done my best to figure out the puzzle.
Serves 8

1 T olive oil
½ c diced pancetta
1 c chopped onion
4 T minced garlic
1 28-oz can crushed tomatoes
1 28-oz can diced tomatoes
½ t salt
½ t red pepper flakes
1 t black pepper
5 or 6 c of chicken broth
2 15-oz cans cannellini beans, drained
1 lb bite-sized pasta, cooked according to
   package directions
1 c grated Romano or Parmesan cheese
½ c fresh basil, chopped
red pepper flakes, for garnish

In a large saucepan, heat the olive oil over medium and sauté the pancetta until it is brown and crispy. With a slotted spoon, remove the pancetta from the pan and reserve it for garnish.

Sauté the onion until translucent. Add the garlic and sauté 4 more minutes. Add the tomatoes, salt, red pepper flakes, and black pepper. Bring the mixture to a simmer and cook for 40 minutes.

Add 5 cups of broth, the beans, and the pasta. Taste and adjust seasonings. If you prefer a thinner soup, add the last cup of broth. Bring the mixture back to a simmer.

Just before serving, stir in the cheese and basil. Sprinkle each serving with the reserved pancetta and additional red pepper flakes, as desired.

Meat Lovers' Cup-o'-Pizza

Our son has voted this hearty soup his favorite. Served with a slice of foccacia, it makes a complete meal that fills up this young man's "hollow leg"—at least for a little while.
Serves 10 (or 4 hungry teenagers)

1 lb spicy Italian sausage
1 lb lean ground beef
2 c coarsely chopped onion
1 lb mushrooms, coarsely chopped
1 medium green bell pepper, diced
1 c chopped zucchini
1 T minced garlic
1 t garlic powder
1 T oregano
1 T basil
1 T dried parsley
2 c canned crushed tomatoes
2 large tomatoes, diced
1 c tomato sauce
4 c beef broth
1 c chopped pepperoni or soppressata
1 c freshly grated mozzarella cheese or small
   mozzarella cheese balls
¼ c grated Parmesan cheese
sliced black olives (optional)

Remove and discard the casing from the sausage. Brown sausage and ground beef in a large saucepan over medium heat. Remove with a slotted spoon and place on a paper-towel–lined plate to drain. Reserve 3 tablespoons of fat in the pan.

Add the onion, mushrooms, green pepper, zucchini, garlic, oregano, basil, and parsley to the pan. Cook for 10 minutes, stirring often. Add the tomatoes, tomato sauce, broth, and pepperoni or soppressata. Return the ground beef and sausage to the pan and stir to combine.

If you're using a slow cooker, cook the soup on low for 6 to 8 hours. If cooking on a stove top, simmer the soup for at least an hour, stirring often.

To serve, top each bowl with the mozzarella and Parmesan cheeses and, if desired, a sprinkle of black olives. If you're using the mozzarella balls, stir them into the bowls of hot soup to create pockets of melted cheese.

CHILLED SOUPS

During the warm summer months, nothing quite quenches our thirst and satisfies our hunger better than a bowl of flavorful chilled soup. Local ingredients picked at the peak of ripeness are the key to cold soups that tempt your taste buds.

Chunky Fresh Gazpacho

One of the easiest recipes you'll find for this refreshing summer classic. Adding the vinegar gives a delicious, subtle tang.
Serves 8 to 10

2 c tomato juice or vegetable juice cocktail
1 c peeled, seeded, finely chopped tomatoes
2 c diced canned tomatoes, with their liquid
1 c finely chopped celery
1 c seeded and finely chopped cucumber
½ c finely chopped red bell pepper
½ c finely chopped Vidalia onion
¼ c finely chopped fresh flat-leaf parsley
3 T red wine vinegar
2 T extra-virgin olive oil
3 large cloves garlic, minced
1 T chopped fresh oregano, or 1 t dried

2 t sugar or Splenda sweetener
1 t salt
1 t Worcestershire sauce
1 t freshly ground black pepper
¼ t cayenne pepper (optional)
10 sprigs fresh parsley, for garnish

Place all of the ingredients except the 10 parsley sprigs in a large stainless steel or glass bowl and mix well. Cover and chill 6 hours or overnight.

Serve cold, garnished with sprigs of parsley.

Shrimp Gazpacho

Gasull is the perfect olive oil for this soup. It's available from Catala Import and Export (see appendix).
Serves 4 to 6

1 European cucumber, peeled and chopped
2 cloves garlic, minced
4 scallions, thinly sliced
1 c finely chopped fresh parsley
1 shallot, minced
2 28-oz cans crushed tomatoes
1 c finely chopped celery
2 t sugar
2 t salt
½ t pepper
3 T red wine vinegar
3 T extra-virgin olive oil, use a fruity variety

1 lb Maine shrimp, cooked

In a food processor, purée the cucumber, garlic, scallions, parsley, and shallot until smooth. Pour mixture into a large bowl and stir in the crushed tomatoes and chopped celery.

In a small bowl, mix the sugar, salt, pepper, vinegar, and oil. Stir into the vegetable mixture. Chill.

Serve in chilled bowls, topping the soup with cooked shrimp. (You can also coarsely chop the shrimp and stir them into the soup. If you do, save out a few whole shrimp for garnish.)

Roasted Pepper and Tomato Soup

Cool and tangy peppers burst into flavor on your tongue.
Serves 4

4 red bell peppers
½ t freshly ground white pepper
10 plum tomatoes
½ t grated gingerroot
3 c chicken broth
⅓ c fresh lemon juice, or to taste
¼ c plain Greek-style yogurt
½ t Maine maple syrup
4 large croutons, for garnish

Roast the peppers as described in the sidebar below.

Chop the peppers coarsely and place them in a large saucepan along with the white pepper, tomatoes, ginger, chicken broth, and lemon juice. Cover and simmer for 40 minutes.

Remove from the heat and set the soup aside to cool.

Either purée the soup in the pan, using an immersion blender. or pour the mixture into a food processor or blender, process until smooth, and return it to the pan.

Stir in the yogurt and maple syrup. Chill the soup for 3 to 4 hours.

Serve in chilled bowls and float a large crouton on top of each bowl.

Roasting Peppers

Preheat the broiler or grill. Have a paper bag on hand large enough to contain the peppers. Cut the peppers in half and remove the stems and seeds.

If using a broiler, place the peppers cut-side down on a greased baking sheet. Broil 3 inches from the heat until the skin blackens. If using a grill, place the peppers skin-side down and roast them until the skin is evenly blackened, turning the peppers often.

Remove the peppers from the grill or broiler pan and place them in the paper bag. Fold the top down to seal and let them steam for 10 to 15 minutes.

Peel the peppers—the skin will come off easily—and they are ready to use in your recipe.

Sweet and Sour Beet Soup with Dilled Sour Cream

Tangy, cool sour cream gives this bright red soup just the right accent. The finest smoked Maine salmon can be ordered from Ducktrap River Fish Farm (see appendix).
Serves 4

8 medium beets, scrubbed well
12 c water
2 c coarsely chopped carrots
1 c chopped celery
2 c chopped red cabbage
2 bay leaves
5 large sprigs dill
6 black peppercorns
1½ t salt
½ c cider vinegar
⅓ c Maine maple syrup or sugar
1 c sour cream
¼ c chopped fresh chives
¼ c chopped fresh dill
½ t black pepper
a few slices of smoked salmon for each serving

Place the beets in a large saucepan and cover with water. Bring to a boil and reduce the heat. Simmer until the beets are fork-tender, about 35 minutes.

Transfer the beets to a bowl, saving the cooking liquid. Peel and coarsely grate the beets when they are cool enough to handle.

Add the carrots, celery, cabbage, bay leaves, dill sprigs, peppercorns, and salt to the saucepan with the beet cooking liquid. Cover and simmer for 30 minutes.

Add the vinegar and maple syrup or sugar to the soup. Stir until the syrup or sugar dissolves. Pour the soup through a fine mesh sieve lined with cheesecloth into a large bowl. Discard the solids. Measure 8 cups of broth, adding water if necessary. Pour the broth back into the saucepan.

Put the sour cream in a bowl and slowly whisk 1 cup of the broth into it until blended. Add the sour cream mixture to the soup, along with the grated beets, chives, and chopped dill. Stir well.

Cool the soup completely, uncovered. Then cover and chill until cold—at least 2 hours.

Season with pepper and salt, to taste. Place a dollop of Dilled Sour Cream atop each bowl of soup. Serve with a few slices of smoked salmon on the side.

Dilled Sour Cream:
Yield: 1 cup
    1 c sour cream
    ¼ c chopped fresh dill

In a small bowl, combine the sour cream and dill.

Strawberry Yogurt Soup with Crunchy Granola Sprinkles

Greek-style yogurt is thicker and richer than other yogurts. It's available at most groceries.
Serves 4

4 c fresh strawberries, sliced
1 c orange juice, freshly squeezed
1 c plain Greek-style yogurt
¼ c Maine maple syrup

Garnish:
   4 pretty whole strawberries
   ½ c of your favorite granola

Place the sliced strawberries into a blender or food processor. Add the orange juice, yogurt, and maple syrup. Purée and pour into small bowls.

   Garnish each bowl with a perfect strawberry and sprinkle with granola.

Blueberry Breakfast Soup

Greet your morning full of energy and antioxidants with this breakfast soup. Wyman's Wild Blueberry Juice—available at most stores—is 100 percent blueberry juice.
Serves 4

3 c Maine blueberries, fresh or frozen
2 c organic vanilla yogurt
3 bananas
2 c blueberry juice
2 T golden flax seeds
¼ c wheat germ
banana slices and whole blueberries, for garnish

Put all ingredients except the garnish in a food processor or blender and pulse until smooth.

   Serve garnished with the banana slices and whole blueberries.

Strawberry Lemongrass Prosecco Soup

Prosecco is a sparkling Italian wine that is usually readily available in stores.

Serves 8 to 12

2 c water
1 3-oz pouch liquid pectin
½ c sugar
1 stalk lemongrass, chopped or grated
6 c strawberries, quartered
2 lemons, juice and zest
4 c prosecco

Garnish:
  6 strawberries
  1 carambola (star fruit), sliced thin
  zest from 1 lemon, finely chopped

Combine the water, pectin, sugar, and lemongrass in a medium saucepan and cook over medium heat, stirring constantly, until the sugar dissolves. Increase the heat and bring the mixture to a boil. Remove from heat.

Purée the strawberries in a blender or food processor. Pour the purée into a large bowl. Set a fine mesh strainer over the bowl and strain the hot lemongrass liquid into the strawberries. Add the grated lemon zest and juice. Adjust the sweetness, if necessary.

Cover the bowl with plastic wrap, and refrigerate 6 hours or overnight.

When you're ready to serve, add the prosecco to the bowl and gently stir to combine. Serve garnished with strawberries, thin slices of star fruit, and a sprinkle of lemon zest.

Apricot Melon Soup with Crystallized Ginger

*C*risp and delicate, this soup is perfect for a summer brunch. If you have some Winterport Winery Cranberry Wine (see appendix), it is wonderful in this recipe.
Serves 8

"Fruit Stock":
1 c pure (not blended) pomegranate juice
1 c pear juice or pear nectar
½ c orange juice, freshly squeezed
½ c seeded and chopped watermelon
½ c sliced strawberries
½ c sliced apricots
1 c sliced bananas
⅓ c lemon or lime juice
¼ to ½ c sweet fruit wine

½ c sliced strawberries
½ c seeded, bite-sized pieces watermelon
½ c seedless grapes
½ c chopped apricots
½ c chopped pineapple chunks
½ c chopped cantaloupe melon
½ c chopped honeydew melon
½ c chopped wintermelon
½ c Maine blueberries, fresh or frozen
¼ c crystallized ginger, finely chopped

Chill eight pretty bowls.

Place all of the "fruit stock" ingredients in a blender and purée until smooth.

Divide the rest of the fresh fruit among the chilled bowls. Pour the "stock" over the fruit. Sprinkle with the crystallized ginger and serve.

Four Berry Soup with Mascarpone Drizzle

This soup is bright, summery, and bursting with flavor. The small, wild Maine berries are sweet and delicious; use locally grown fresh berries whenever you can. Mascarpone is a soft Italian cream cheese. If you cannot find mascarpone, substitute softened cream cheese mixed with a tablespoon of whipping cream.
Serves 4

4 c sliced strawberries, slightly frozen
2 c fresh raspberries, chilled
1½ c vanilla yogurt
½ c heavy cream
1 lemon, juice and zest
3 T Maine maple syrup, or more to taste
1 c fresh blackberries, chilled
1 c fresh Maine blueberries, chilled

Place the strawberries and half of the raspberries into a blender or food processor and purée until

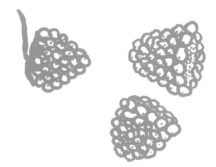

smooth. Add 1 cup of the yogurt and the heavy cream. Purée again until free of lumps. Add the rest of the yogurt, lemon juice, zest, and maple syrup, and blend again briefly.

Taste and sweeten if necessary. Chill.

To serve, pour the berry soup into shallow bowls and dot with the remaining raspberries and the blackberries and blueberries.

Spoon a pretty design on each bowl with the Mascarpone Drizzle.

Mascarpone Drizzle:
Yield: about ⅓ cup
    ¼ c mascarpone cheese
    2 T Maine maple syrup
    ½ t pure vanilla extract

In a small saucepan, melt the mascarpone over low heat. Stir in the maple syrup and vanilla. Let cool to room temperature.

DESSERT SOUPS

Sweet soups are a refreshing way to enjoy dessert. Capture the flavor of fruit, chocolate, or custard in a soup, add an interesting texture, and you've got a delightful way to amuse your mouth.

Liquid Cinnamon Chocolate with Brown Sugar Espresso Cream

Cinnamon and espresso enhance the flavor of chocolate in this warm, luscious soup.
Serves 4

2 c milk
2 c light cream
2 3- to 4-inch cinnamon sticks, broken in half
4 T instant espresso powder
6 T dark brown sugar, packed
½ c unsweetened cocoa powder
1 c chopped milk chocolate
nutmeg and additional cinnamon sticks,
    for garnish

Simmer milk, cream, and cinnamon sticks in a medium saucepan over low heat until bubbles form around the edges of the pan.

Whisk in the espresso powder, brown sugar, and cocoa. Add the milk chocolate and whisk until it melts and the soup is smooth. Discard the cinnamon sticks.

Ladle into four heat-proof bowls. Top with Brown Sugar Espresso Cream and sprinkle with nutmeg. Garnish with additional cinnamon sticks, if desired.

Brown Sugar Espresso Cream:
Yield: about 1 cup
    ½ c heavy cream, chilled
    4 t light brown sugar, packed
    2 t instant espresso powder
    ½ t pure vanilla extract

Whip the cream in a medium bowl until soft peaks form. Sprinkle in the brown sugar, espresso powder, and vanilla and continue whipping until stiff.

Cover and refrigerate until ready to use.

Choco-Mocha-Latte Soup

A strongly flavored, coffee-infused cream embraces the sweet, dark chocolate in this rich soup. Excellent espresso beans and ground coffee can be found at Coffee by Design (see appendix).
Serves 4

4 T freshly ground espresso beans
2 c heavy cream
2 c dark chocolate bits
2 oz unsweetened chocolate, chopped

Garnish:
  chocolate-covered espresso beans
  2 T heavy cream

In a small saucepan, heat the ground espresso and 2 cups of heavy cream together over low heat until bubbles form around the edges of the pan.

Remove from the heat and let stand for 5 minutes to infuse the cream with the flavor of espresso. Pour the cream through a fine-mesh sieve lined with a coffee filter into a clean, small saucepan. Whisk in the chocolate bits and unsweetened choclate pieces and stir until they melt. (If necessary, place the pan over very low heat and stir constantly until the chocolate becomes liquid.)

Serve this soup warm, garnished with chocolate-covered espresso beans and drops of heavy cream floated on the surface. If you gently drag a toothpick through the entire drop of cream (right through the middle), it will form a pretty heart.

Warm Chocolate Silk with Fresh Strawberries and White Chocolate Curls

Use the best cocoa you can find for this thick chocolate soup. The cocoa nibs (bits of toasted cocoa bean) add crunch .
Serves 4

1 c premium cocoa powder (such as Ghirardelli or Scharffen Berger), sifted
1¼ c water
1½ c granulated sugar
1 c heavy cream
1 c chopped semisweet chocolate

Garnish:
  8 fresh strawberries, sliced
  white chocolate curls
  4 T cocoa nibs (optional)

In a medium, heavy-bottomed saucepan, whisk the cocoa with the water over medium heat. Bring to a simmer and cook until thick.

Add the sugar and whisk until it dissolves. Add the heavy cream and chopped chocolate. Whisk until the chocolate melts completely.

Serve warm, garnished with sliced fresh strawberries, white chocolate curls, and, if desired, the cocoa nibs.

Warm White Chocolate Alexander Soup

Creamy and spiked with brandy, this white chocolate delight will take the chill off.
Serves 4

4 c light cream
6 egg yolks
3 c finely chopped white chocolate
¼ c brandy, spiced rum, or Grand Marnier
1 t vanilla extract
dark and white chocolate curls, for garnish

Heat light cream in a medium saucepan over medium heat until bubbles form around the edges.

While the cream is heating, whisk the egg yolks in a bowl. When the cream is hot, pour ½ cup into the eggs, whisking constantly. Pour the eggs and cream back into the pan and whisk over low heat until the mixture is thick.

Remove the pan from the heat. Add the white chocolate, your choice of liquor, and the vanilla. Whisk until the soup is completely smooth. Serve garnished with chocolate curls.

Sugar-Free Chocolate Lava

Thick, hot, and chocolatey, this soup is sugar-free—but you would never know it. If you want to use sugar instead, substitute the same amount of sugar for the Splenda sweetener.
Serves 4 to 6

1½ c cocoa powder
2 c milk
½ t cinnamon or 1½ t espresso powder
¾ c Splenda sweetener
1 t vanilla

In a heavy saucepan, combine the cocoa, milk, and cinnamon or espresso powder. Whisk until thoroughly combined. Bring the mixture to a boil over medium heat. Cook, stirring often, for 5 minutes or until the soup is thick.

Cool 10 minutes. Add the Splenda and vanilla.

Melted Snowman Soup

This one is great fun for kids as they each assemble their own "melted snowman."
Serves 4

4 individual serving size packages hot cocoa powder
16 Hershey's Kisses chocolates
32 miniature marshmallows
4 small candy canes
4 c milk

Set out four mugs and spoons. Ask each child to prepare a mug: empty 1 package of cocoa powder into the mug and add 4 Kisses, 8 marshmallows, and 1 candy cane.

Heat the milk over medium heat until bubbles form around the edge of the pan. Pour hot milk into each child's mug. Ask the children to stir carefully and enjoy their soup with a spoon.

Peaches and Cream Soup with Cinnamon Slivers

Roasting the peaches makes them even sweeter. For the Cinnamon Slivers, use your favorite pastry dough recipe (enough for a single pie crust), or the version below.
Serves 4

4 large peaches, peeled and cut in half
1½ c light brown sugar, packed
2 c peach nectar
1 t pure vanilla extract
1 c orange juice, freshly squeezed
2 lemons, juice and zest
4 T peach liqueur
2 T Triple Sec
½ c heavy cream

Garnish:
  1 c strawberries, sliced
  2 sprigs mint

Preheat the oven to 350 degrees F. Coat the peach halves with light brown sugar. (Reserve the remaining sugar.) Place the peaches cut-side down in a greased 9 by 11–inch baking dish. Bake the peaches for 30 minutes. Cool.

Place the baked peaches in a food processor or blender, along with any juice from the baking dish. Purée until smooth. Add the reserved brown sugar and 1 cup of peach nectar and purée again until smooth. Pour into a bowl and stir in the remaining peach nectar, vanilla, orange juice, lemon juice and zest, peach liqueur, and Triple Sec. Add the heavy cream and stir. Chill until ready to serve.

Garnish with sliced strawberries, sprigs of mint, and serve with Cinnamon Slivers on the side.

Cinnamon Slivers:
Yield: 8 pieces
  1⅛ c all-purpose flour
  1½ t sugar
  ½ t salt
  4 T unsalted butter, chilled, in ¼-inch pieces
  1 T solid vegetable shortening
  1 to 2 T ice water
  1 T butter, melted
  3 T light brown sugar, packed
  1 T cinnamon

Sift together the flour, sugar, and salt. Using your fingers, work in the butter and shortening until the mixture resembles coarse crumbs.

Add 1 T of the ice water and work the dough with your fingers until the water is incorporated. Sprinkle in more water as needed until the dough comes together, being careful not to overmix. Form the dough into a disk, wrap it tightly in plastic wrap, and refrigerate for at least 30 minutes.

Preheat oven to 400 degrees F. Roll out the pastry ¼ inch thick on a parchment-lined sheet pan. Brush the dough with the melted butter.

In a small bowl, mix the brown sugar and cinnamon until uniform in color. Sprinkle the mixture over the dough.

Using a rolling pastry or pizza cutter, divide the pastry into 8 slivers. Bake 25 minutes or until the bottom of the crust is lightly browned.

Raspberry Chambord Soup

This is the epitome of a romantic dessert. The "blush-ing" raspberries burst with flavor in the middle of a velvety white chocolate "kiss."
Serves 4

2 c finely chopped white chocolate
2 c heavy cream
1 t vanilla extract
⅓ c Chambord liqueur
1 c fresh raspberries
white chocolate curls, for garnish

Place the white chocolate in an ovenproof glass bowl. In a medium saucepan, heat the cream over medium heat until bubbles form around the edge of the pan. Remove from the heat and gradually stir one quarter of the hot cream into the chocolate. Whisk until the chocolate melts. Add the remaining hot cream mixture and the vanilla to the melted chocolate, stirring constantly.

Stir in the Chambord and ½ cup of the raspberries.

Pour into pretty bowls or wide-mouthed champagne glasses. Top with the remaining raspberries and chocolate curls and serve immediately.

Pomegranate and Champagne Soup with Kiwi Medallions

Crisp and refreshing: This soup is the perfect end to a meal on a hot summer night.
Serves 4 to 6

4 c pomegranate juice
3 oz liquid pectin
½ c sugar
2 limes, juice and zest
seeds from 1 pomegranate
1 c pomegranate liqueur
2 c dry champagne

Garnish:
 4 kiwi, peeled and thinly sliced
 pomegranate seeds

In a medium saucepan, bring the pomegranate juice, pectin, and sugar to a boil. Lower the heat and simmer until the sugar completely dissolves.

Remove from the heat and add the lime juice and zest. Let cool and chill at least 8 hours.

Remove the seeds from the pomegranate. An easy way to do this is to submerge the pomegranate in a large bowl of water in the sink. Cut off the top and bottom of the fruit. Break the pomegranate open and gently work the seeds out of the membrane. They should easily come out in the water bath; the seeds will sink to the bottom of the bowl and any excess membrane will float. Discard all membrane and drain the seeds in a colander.

When you're ready to serve, gently stir the pomegranate liqueur and champagne into the thickened soup. Place 20 or so seeds in each bowl, reserving the rest for garnish. Top with the soup. Garnish with medallions of kiwi and a few additional pomegranate seeds.

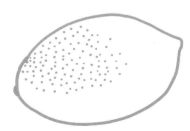

OVER THE TOP AND ON THE SIDE

Turning a bowl of soup into a satisfying meal is easy—just add dumplings, top it with a crisp crust, or serve it with a slice of quick bread or a warm biscuit spread with a sweet and savory chutney. Here are a few tricks you can pull out of your sleeve to wow your family.

Pastry Toppings for Soup

For a change, you can top your soup with pastry rather than serving bread on the side. Make the basic pastry dough from the Cinnamon Slivers recipe on page 90 or use your own favorite pie cust recipe—enough to make a single 9- or 10-inch crust. One of the tricks to a flaky crust is using very cold butter and ice water. To ensure a tender crust, make the dough ahead of time and let it rest, chilled, for at least 30 minutes (or up to 24 hours) before rolling it out.

To make a pot pie:

Many of the thick soups and stews in this book can be adapted for pot pie filling by reducing the amount of liquid slightly.

Preheat oven to 400 degrees F. Pour warm thick soup into a deep casserole dish. Cover the top with rolled-out pastry dough. Trim to fit. (Use your favorite recipe or the Cinnamon Slivers pastry dough on p. 90, without the cinnamon-sugar topping.)

Cut several slits in the pastry to allow steam to escape. Place the casserole on a pizza pan or baking sheet to catch any bubble-overs, and bake until pastry is golden, approximately 20 minutes.

To make floaters:

An alternative is to top individual bowls of soup with pastry "floaters" baked separately.

Preheat oven to 400 degrees F. Using your favorite pastry dough or the recipe on p. 90 (without the cinnamon-sugar topping), roll out the dough to ¼-inch thick. Place the sheet of dough onto the baking sheet and cut it into wedges or squares. Bake until the pastry is golden, approximately 20 minutes.

Float a piece of warm, flaky crust atop each bowl of hot soup, and serve.

For an herb crust:

Add 2 T of chopped fresh herbs to the recipe for a single pie crust. (If making a double recipe, use ¼ c of fresh herbs.)

I like to use parsley and rosemary, but many combinations are possible. Just remember to take into consideration what flavors are in the accompanying soup.

Be extra careful when rolling out an herb dough, as the crust can tear more easily than plain pastry does.

For a sweet crust:

Add 1½ t of Maine maple syrup to the recipe for a single pie crust. ¼ t of cinnamon is a delicious addition as well—mix it in with the dry ingredients.

(If making a double recipe, use 1 T maple syrup and ½ t cinnamon.)

Matzo Balls

Great in chicken soup, of course, but try these cousins of dumplings in other soups and stews as well.
Serves 10

¼ c oil
4 eggs, lightly beaten
1 c matzo meal
1 t Maine sea salt
¼ t ground ginger
¼ t onion powder
¼ c water
3 T finely chopped parsley

In a medium bowl, combine the oil and eggs. Add the matzo meal, salt, ginger, and onion powder. Mix well. Stir in the water and parsley. Chill, covered, for 30 minutes.

Bring a pot of water to a boil. Form the matzo mixture into 1-inch balls and drop them into boiling water. Cover and cook over low heat 30 to 35 minutes. Remove the matzo balls from the pot with a slotted spoon and place into hot soup.

Asiago Lace Cornets

These, lacy cheese crisps are rolled into cornets when they are still warm. If desired, they can also be served as flat rounds.
Yield: 1 dozen

8 oz fresh Asiago cheese, coarsely grated

Preheat oven to 325 degrees F.

Line a baking sheet with parchment paper or a Silpat silicone sheet. Place a mounded tablespoon of Asiago on the liner. Shape the cheese into a 2-inch circle. Repeat this process with the remaining cheese, leaving a 2-inch space between circles.

Bake 5 to 6 minutes, or until bubbly and lightly golden. Quickly remove each cheese round with a spatula and gently shape it into a cone. If the rounds become too brittle to shape, simply put them back into the hot oven for a minute or so to soften.

Parmesan Garlic Wafers

Parmesan and garlic are a match made in heaven. Look for the classic Parmigiano-Reggiano for this recipe.
Yield: approximately 14 wafers

10 oz fresh Parmigiano-Reggiano cheese,
   coarsely grated
¼ t garlic powder

Place an oven rack in the middle of the oven and preheat oven to 350° degrees F. Line a baking sheet with parchment paper or a Silpat.

   Mix the cheese and garlic powder together in a small bowl. Place heaping tablespoons of the cheese in mounds 4 inches apart on the baking sheet. Spread the mounds evenly into 3-inch ovals. Bake the Parmesan wafers approximately 8 to 10 minutes, or until the cheese is golden and crisp.

   Remove from the oven and cool the wafers completely on the baking sheet. Remove the cooled wafers carefully with a spatula.

   They can be made up to a day in advance. Store between layers of parchment paper in a sealed container at room temperature.

Croutons

Toasty slices of bread are the perfect accompaniment to soup.

crusty French bread, one to two slices
   per serving
jam, butter, or salad dressing (optional)
fresh parsley, chopped (optional)

Lightly toast the slices of French bread. Float them atop your soup — plain or slathered with a little jam, butter, salad dressing, pesto, salsa, or chutney and sprinkled with parsley.

Cereal Party Mix

This family snack favorite tastes great as a soup topper.
Yield: 6 cups

1 c toasted oat cereal
1 c wheat cereal squares
1 c rice cereal squares
1 c corn cereal squares
2 c thin, short pretzel sticks
¼ c melted butter
½ t Worcestershire sauce
¼ t celery salt
¼ t garlic salt
dash cayenne pepper

Preheat the oven to 250 degrees F.

Mix the cereals and pretzel sticks together in a large bowl. Combine the melted butter and seasonings. Pour over the cereal mix and stir well to coat.

Spread in a single layer on a baking sheet and bake for an hour, stirring every 15 minutes.

Cajun Spiced Pecans

Great for topping a soup or serving on the side.
Serves 6 to 8

1 lb pecan halves
¼ c butter, melted
1 T chili powder
1 t salt
1 t basil
1 t oregano
1 t thyme
½ t onion powder
½ t garlic powder
¼ to ½ t cayenne pepper, to taste

Preheat oven to 400 degrees F.

Combine all ingredients in a shallow baking dish and bake for 15 minutes.

Stir and reduce heat to 250 degrees. Cook, stirring every 15 minutes, for one hour.

Remove from oven and cool completely.

Cheese and Bacon Muffins

State of Maine Cheese Company's Saco Jalapeño is delicious in this recipe (see appendix).
Yield: 1 dozen

2 c unbleached flour
2½ t baking powder
1 t salt
6 slices bacon, fried crisp, drained, and crumbled
1¼ c shredded pepper Jack cheese
⅓ c snipped chives
2 eggs
1 c milk
2 t Maine maple syrup
1 T coarse-grained Dijon mustard
5 T butter, melted

Preheat oven to 400 degrees F. Line a 12-cup muffin tin with paper liners.

Sift the flour, baking powder, and salt into a large bowl. Stir in the bacon, cheese, and chives.

Lightly beat the eggs with the milk and maple syrup until well blended. Whisk in the mustard and butter. Add the egg mixture to the dry ingredients and stir just until blended.

Spoon the batter into the prepared muffin cups. Bake 15 to 20 minutes, or until golden brown. Let cool for a few minutes before serving.

Tomatillo Cheddar Corn Bread

Green tomatillos speckle this moist and spicy corn bread.
Serves 12 generously

3 c yellow cornmeal
1 c flour
4 t baking powder
2 t baking soda
1 T salt
1 t cayenne pepper
3 c buttermilk
6 T Maine maple syrup or sugar
4 eggs
6 T butter, melted
2 c shredded sharp cheddar cheese
½ c tomatillo salsa

Preheat oven to 425 degrees F. Grease two 9-inch cake pans or pie plates.

In a large bowl, combine the cornmeal, flour, baking powder, baking soda, salt, and cayenne pepper. Stir to mix well.

In another bowl, whisk together the buttermilk, maple syrup, eggs, and butter. Gently fold the wet ingredients into the dry ingredients, stirring just until combined. Fold in the cheese and salsa.

Fill the prepared pans or pie plates. Bake for 30 minutes, until the centers are firm and the tops are golden. Cool before slicing.

Blue Cheese Apple Butter Puff

Try Pastor Chuck's Organic Apple Butter in this recipe (see appendix). It features the concentrated flavor of apples and fresh, complementary spices.
Serves 8

2 sheets puff pastry, thawed if frozen
4 T apple butter
8 oz blue cheese, crumbled
1 egg, lightly beaten

Preheat oven to 400 degrees F.

Unfold the puff pastry sheets and place each on a parchment- or Silpat-lined sheet pan. Gently press the seams together where the pastry was folded. Brush each sheet with 2 tablespoons of apple butter and sprinkle with half of the blue cheese.

Refold the pastry sheets the way they were folded in the package. Then fold the left third of each pastry bundle toward the center and fold the right third over the top of that, creating a narrow rectangle for each piece of pastry.

Brush each rectangle with the beaten egg. Bake for 15 to 20 minutes, or until the tops are puffed and lightly browned.

Remove the puffs from the oven and let them cool 10 minutes. Place the puffs on a cutting board and carefully slice each puff into 8 pieces with a serrated knife.

Rosemary Chèvre Soda Bread

There is something magical about the blended flavors of rosemary and goat cheese. They come together in this quick bread to complement your meal. Appleton Creamery's chèvre is delicious in this recipe (see appendix).
Serves 12

4 c King Arthur all-purpose flour
1 T baking powder
1 t baking soda
½ t salt
¼ t freshly ground cardamom
1 T chopped fresh rosemary
¾ c plain chèvre
3 eggs, lightly beaten
¼ c Maine maple syrup
1½ c buttermilk
2 T butter, melted
3 T butter, chilled

Preheat oven to 350 degrees F. Grease a sheet pan.

In a large bowl, combine the flour, baking powder, baking soda, salt, cardamom, and rosemary.

In another bowl, stir together the chèvre, eggs, maple syrup, buttermilk, and melted butter. Stir the wet ingredients into the flour mixture.

Turn out onto a floured surface and knead gently for 3 minutes or until the dough is smooth. Divide the dough into two pieces, shaping each into a round loaf. Place each half in a greased 8-inch cake pan or pie plate, pressing it down until the dough fills the pan or plate.

Use a sharp knife to cut a ½-inch-deep cross on the top of each loaf. Dot the loaves with the 3 tablespoons of chilled butter.

Bake for about 40 minutes, or until the bread sounds hollow when you tap the tops. Turn out onto a wire rack to cool. Cut in wedges to serve.

Blueberry Pumpkin Bread

The combination of pumpkin and blueberries is delightful. Molasses keeps the bread moist and delicious. Toast a slice of this bread and spread it with a whisper of fresh butter. It's a great accompaniment to a cup of soup.
Makes 2 loaves

4 c King Arthur all-purpose flour
1 t baking powder
2 t baking soda
1 t cinnamon
½ t nutmeg
1 t salt
¾ c molasses
⅔ c sugar
½ c unsweetened applesauce
½ c oil
4 large eggs, lightly beaten
2 c canned pumpkin
¼ c apple cider
1½ c fresh or frozen blueberries

Preheat oven to 350 degrees F. Grease and flour two medium loaf pans.

In a medium bowl, combine the flour, baking powder, baking soda, cinnamon, nutmeg, and salt.

In a separate bowl, combine the molasses, sugar, applesauce, oil, eggs, pumpkin, and cider. Mix well. Add the dry ingredients and stir to combine. Gently fold in the blueberries.

Spoon the batter into the prepared loaf pans. Bake until a toothpick inserted in the centers of the loaves comes out clean, about 1 hour.

Cool the bread in the pans for about 10 minutes, then turn the loaves out of the pans onto a wire rack to cool completely.

APPENDIX

Specialty Products from Maine Producers

Appleton Creamery
780 Gurney Town Road, Appleton, ME 04862
Web site: www.appletoncreamery.com
E-mail: info@appletoncreamery.com

The creamery's award-winning chèvre comes in a variety of sizes and flavors. "Our chèvre is brought to market within days of being made."

Borealis Breads
P.O. Box 1800, Wells, ME 04090-1800
Phone: (207) 641-8800
Web site: www.borealisbreads.com
E-mail: info@borealisbreads.com

The Van Gogh of dough is this artisanal bakery's slogan. *"This is bread made the way it has been made for millennia."*

Catala Import and Export
P.O. Box 143, West Boothbay Harbor, ME 04575
Web site: www.catalaimports.com
E-mail: CatalaImportandExport@aol.com

Catala's Gasull Extra Virgin Olive Oil is a delicious cold-pressed oil from Spain.

Coffee by Design
43 Washington Avenue, Portland, ME 04101
Phone: (207) 879-2233
Web site: www.coffeebydesign.com
E-mail: javainfo@coffeebydesign.com
"Our mission is to educate people about specialty coffee and to provide them with the best quality coffee beans."

Ducktrap River Fish Farm
57 Little River Drive, Belfast, ME 04915
Phone: (207) 338-6280 or (800) 828-3825
Web site: www.ducktrap.com
E-mail: smoked@ducktrap.com

Ducktrap's mission is "to wow each customer with quality one bite at a time. Excellent smoked seafood, every time."

Goranson Farm
Jan Goranson and Rob Johanson
250 River Road, Dresden, Maine 04342
Phone: (207) 737-8834
Web site: http://home.gwi.net/~goransonfarm
  /index.htm
E-mail: goransonfarm@gwi.net

"For generations we have had an on-farm market providing high-quality specialty potatoes and a large variety of other vegetables, our maple syrup, and locally produced meats."

Maine Gold Maple Syrup and Gifts
229 Park Street, Rockland, ME 04841
Phone: (800) 752-5271
Web site: www.mainegold.com
E-mail: webmanagement@mainegold.com

"100 percent pure, award winning maple syrup from Maine. We send gift baskets around the world, filled with Maine Gold Maple Syrup and goodies."

Pastor Chuck Orchards
P.O. Box 1259, Portland, ME 04104
Phone: (207) 773-1314
Web site: www.pastorchuckorchards.com
E-mail: waite@pastorchuckorchards.com
Pastor Chuck's organic apple butter and apple-sauce are available at specialty food shops and via their Web site.

Quoddy Mist
L&C Enterprise LLC
72 Water Street, Lubec, ME 04652
Phone: (207) 733-4847
Web site: www.quoddymist.com
E-mail: info@quoddymist.com

Producer of "an all-natural, high-quality sea salt in a variety of grades, crystal sizes, and flavors."

Rising Tide Cooperative Market Health Store
15 Coastal Market Place, Damariscotta, ME 04543
Phone: (207) 563-5556
Web site: www.risingtide.coop

Rising Tide provided some of the food used for testing the soup recipes in this book. "A member-owned natural foods cooperative committed to providing local, natural, and organic food to the Mid-Coast community."

Sheepscot River Pottery
34 U.S. Route 1, Edgecomb, ME 04578
Phone: (207) 882-9410
Web site: www.sheepscot.com
E-mail: SheepscotRiverPottery@verizon.net

Sheepscot pottery is shown in several of the photographs in this book. "Our clay body is unique, our firing cycle is unique, and our designs are definitely unique—no other potter does what we do."

Sheepscot Valley Brewing Company
74 Hollywood Boulevard, Whitefield, ME 04353
Phone: (207) 549-5530
Web site: www.sheepscotbrewing.com
E-mail: BrewSteve@photo-ne.com

"Owner and brewer Steve Gorrill homebrewed for ten years prior to establishing the micro-brewery in April of 1995." Tours available.

Shipwreck Galley Spirited Salsa
P.O. Box 373, Presque Isle, ME 04769
Phone: (207) 762-1001
Web site: www.shipwreckgalley.com
E-mail: pegleg@shipwreckgalley.com

"Unique combinations of spirit and spice intensify the flavor to tingle the taste buds."

State of Maine Cheese Company
461 Commercial St., Rockport, ME 04856
Phone: (207) 236-8895
Web site: www.cheese-me.com
E-mail: admin@cheese-me.com

Hand-crafted cheeses and fresh cheese curd without the addition of preservatives or colorings. "We use milk from Maine farms that choose not to use artificial growth hormones."

Winterport Winery
279 South Main St., Winterport, ME 04496
Phone: (207) 223-4500
Web site: www.winterportwinery.com
E-mail: info@winterportwinery.com

"Our award-winning wines are fermented and aged under the careful supervision of Head Winemaker Michael Anderson."

INDEX

Index